Primary mathematics | **Whole-class intera**

The big interactive book o

shape and >>>

>>> measuring

4

AGES 8 – 9

< **Understanding shape**

Measuring >

Activities for every objective of
the NEW Primary Framework
for Mathematics in both digital
and book format.

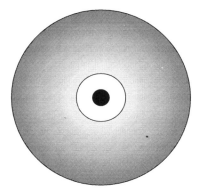

6048UK

Published by Prim-Ed Publishing 2007
Copyright© Clare Way 2004
ISBN 978 1 84654 092 9
PR–6048

Titles available in this series:

Copyright statement

The objectives have been taken from the 'Primary National Strategy – Primary Framework for literacy and mathematics', 2006. Reproduced under the terms of the Click-Use Licence.

Internet websites

In some cases, websites or specific URLs may be recommended. While these are checked and rechecked at the time of publication, the publisher has no control over any subsequent changes which may be made to webpages. It is *strongly* recommended that the class teacher checks *all* URLs before allowing pupils to access them.

View all pages online

Email address: sales@prim-ed.com   Home page: http://www.prim-ed.com

Foreword

Primary mathematics is a photocopiable, six-level, year-specific series designed to address the **Primary Framework for Mathematics** objectives of:

- using and applying mathematics
- counting and understanding number
- knowing and using number facts
- calculating
- understanding shape
- measuring
- handling data.

Each book in the **Primary mathematics** series includes:

- at least one activity page for each objective
- comprehensive teachers notes to accompany each activity
- additional teachers notes on activities and games
- assessment checklists
- additional photocopiable resources
- interactive whiteboard resources on accompanying disk.

The Year 4 books in the **Primary mathematics** series are:

Primary mathematics – Using and applying maths/Calculating

Primary mathematics – Counting and understanding number/Knowing and
using number facts/Handling data

Primary mathematics – Understanding shape/Measuring

Contents

Teachers notes

Using interactive resources

The **Primary mathematics** series provides teachers with a number of varied and challenging activities. It also provides the teacher with a range of choices in selecting an appropriate medium to present these activities. These are:

(i)   traditional print medium, where the teacher uses the copymasters provided to support and develop the objective being taught

(ii) interactive medium, where the teacher uses the interactive resources provided to engage the pupils in activities presented through an interactive whiteboard

(iii) digital activities, where the teacher uses the copymasters provided in a digital format, utilising management tools to focus on different areas of the activity

(iv) any combination of the above.

The **Primary mathematics** series is a comprehensive mathematics resource. The resources are provided in two formats which can be used independently or in a combined manner. These are:

(i)   *Print format:* this format is represented by this book. The structure is explained in the table of contents and comprises teachers notes and pupil activities to support each objective of the **Primary Framework for Mathematics**.

(ii) *Digital format:* this format provides all of the resources of the *Print format* and supplements this further by providing specific interactive activities to support the teaching of objectives, where appropriate. It also provides teacher information and pupil activity pages in a digital format that is easily accessed from a laptop computer and which provides a new range of teaching methods and strategies for using traditional copymasters.

The following notes outline the features and uses of the *Digital format* of this resource.

From the digital resource teachers can access and use:

(i)   Teachers notes in digital format

(ii) Interactive activities

(iii) Copymasters in digital format

These are accessed through an easy-to-use navigation system.

Navigation

Click on the logo to go to teacher support for how to use the book/interactive, setting up a maths classroom, activities and games, assessment checklists and additional resources.

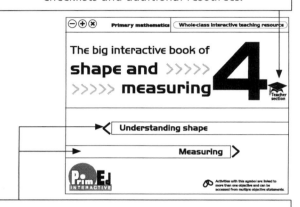

Choose a curriculum strand by clicking on it.

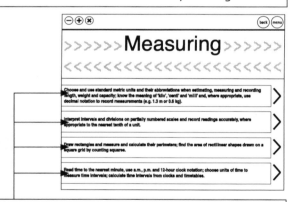

Click on an objective to see the related activities.

Activities with this symbol are linked to multiple objectives.

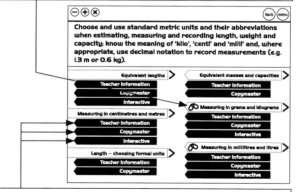

Click to go to the related: • teacher information
• copymaster
• interactive activity

Teachers notes

Using interactive resources

Digital teachers notes

The notes provided in this section are identical to the notes provided in print format in this book. The purpose of providing them digitally is to allow:

(i)   ease of access for the teacher in the planning stage

(ii)   ease of access for the teacher during the lesson.

Interactive activities

In each book of the **Primary mathematics** series specific activities have been provided in an interactive format. The purpose of these activities is to support the teacher in explaining and demonstrating specific objectives. The interactive format provides demonstration capacity and also a practice activity for whole-class, small group and individual pupil teaching.

Digital copymasters

Providing the copymaster activity in digital format is more than just a printed page on a digital file. We have added management tools to aid the teacher in using the activity page on the interactive whiteboard. The features of this new format include:

(i)   print the file direct to a printer if you wish to make multiple copies

(ii)   the page can be displayed and pupils can complete answers directly from the whiteboard - reducing the level of photocopying required

(iii) the page can be zoomed in or out, allowing the teacher to concentrate attention on a specific activity – also reducing the distraction of other activities being displayed

(iv)   the teacher can use screens provided to blank out certain sections of the page to isolate a teaching or learning point

(v)   the page can be moved around the screen

(vi)   answers can be written onto the screen in a format related to the specific design of different whiteboard manufacturers.

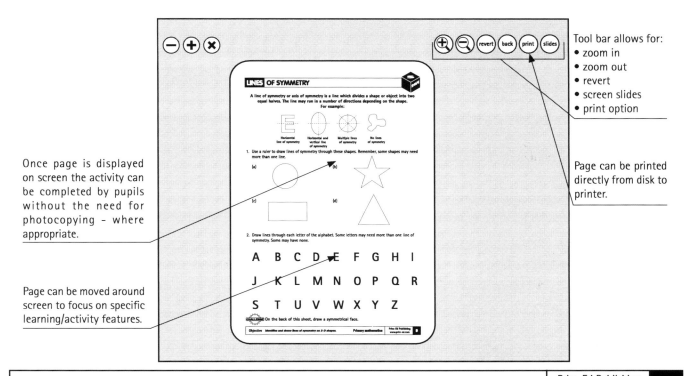

Tool bar allows for:
• zoom in
• zoom out
• revert
• screen slides
• print option

Once page is displayed on screen the activity can be completed by pupils without the need for photocopying - where appropriate.

Page can be moved around screen to focus on specific learning/activity features.

Page can be printed directly from disk to printer.

Teachers notes

How to use this book

The **Primary mathematics** series provides teachers with a number of varied and challenging activities. At least one activity, often more, is provided for each objective of the **Primary Framework for Mathematics**.

Suggestions for using the activities in this book:

Objective:

- *Decide which curriculum objective you wish to address and choose the appropriate activity page(s).*

Oral work and mental calculation starter:

- *Choose which oral and mental activities you will use, from the list provided, to introduce the lesson or sharpen pupils' skills.*

- *Some of the activities have accompanying interactive whiteboard activities to help introduce the lesson and capture pupils' attention.*

- *These activities should occupy the first 5–10 minutes of the lesson.*

Main teaching activity:

- *Decide how much teacher input you will provide for the main activity and whether pupils will be working individually, in pairs or as a group.*

- *Depending upon the abilities of the pupils in your class, decide whether any additional activities will be needed, from the list provided, or whether these can be used during subsequent lessons.*

- *This activity should occupy approximately 40 minutes.*

Plenary:

- *Decide what opportunities will be provided during the plenary session. Will pupils be given the opportunity to share and explain work, compare strategies used or summarise the key facts they have learnt?*

- *Think about how you can use the plenary session to assess pupils' progress and therefore inform your future planning.*

- *The plenary should occupy the final 15 minutes of the lesson.*

Pupil activity pages:

The pupil activities follow a common format:

Title explanation

After initial discussion, some activities can be completed individually, and others in small groups or as a whole class.

The 'Challenge' activity can be completed by early finishers or those pupils requiring extension of the task. Pupils may need to complete the activity on the back of the worksheet or investigate an activity further by using concrete materials or creating their own ideas linked to the objective.

The objective provides the teacher with the focus of the activity. It is written in the form of a general objective.

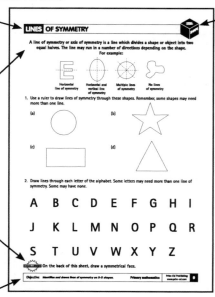

An icon denotes the curriculum strand for each activity.

 Using and applying mathematics

 Counting and understanding number

 Knowing and using number facts

 Calculating

 Understanding shape

 Measuring

 Handling data

Teachers notes

How to use this book

Teachers pages

A teachers page accompanies each pupil worksheet. It provides the following information:

The **objective** tells the teacher which strand and objective from the **Primary Framework for Mathematics** is being covered.

Oral work and mental calculation activities are suggested, for introducing the lesson or sharpening/developing oral and mental skills. The activities should occupy the first 10 minutes of the lesson.

Some activities have **interactive whiteboard activities** on the accompanying disk. If an interactive activity is provided it is listed here.

The title of the **main teaching activity** is given. The photocopiable activity is on the page facing the teachers notes. The main activity should occupy approximately 40 minutes.

Suggestions for **additional activities** are provided. They can be completed during the lesson, or in subsequent lessons. They can be used to aid differentiation.

Answers to all activities are provided.

Assessment

Assessment checklists have been included for the Year 4 'Understanding shape' and 'Measuring' objectives. See pages x–xi. These can be used to assess each pupil's understanding of the key objectives covered.

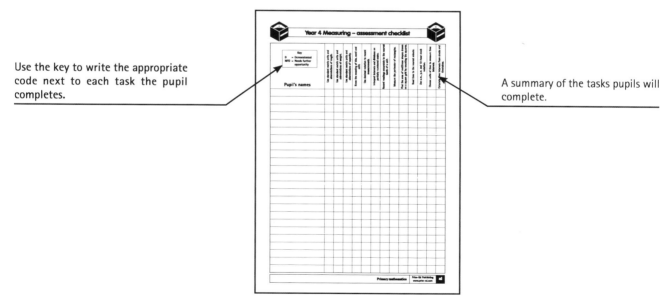

Use the key to write the appropriate code next to each task the pupil completes.

A summary of the tasks pupils will complete.

- *Teaching notes for the 'Understanding shape' and 'Measuring' strands have been included on page ix. They comprise background information and suggested activities and games.*

- *Extra teacher resources have been included on pages xii–xvii. These can be enlarged if necessary and used in appropriate activities or as display posters.*

- *Interactive whiteboard activities have been provided to help teach some of the objectives. These can be found on the accompanying disk.*

Teachers notes

Setting up a mathematics classroom

By having the following materials and visual representations around them, pupils can better engage in mathematical learning.

- *Allow room to move so pupils can investigate things around the room. Organise desks and floor space appropriately.*

- *Display a 'Numbers' chart.*

- *Display a number line at a level where pupils can use it. Include negative numbers on the number line.*

- *Display numbers, number words and a visual representation of numbers.*

- *Display addition and subtraction facts.*

- *Display a 100 square.*

- *Ensure you have a good range of maths games and use them regularly.*

- *Provide calculators.*

- *Display 'times tables' charts.*

- *Have an analogue and digital clock in the classroom.*

- *Display pictures of labelled 2-D and 3-D shapes.*

- *Provide construction materials such as cardboard boxes, cylinders, paper, scissors and so on.*

- *Ensure you have adequate concrete materials to teach each strand (refer to page ix).*

- *Allow pupils opportunities to investigate outside the classroom in the school environment.*

- *Display posters of fractions.*

- *Display a chart showing equivalent fractions and decimals.*

- *Display or make various graphs such as pictograms, bar charts, block graphs, Venn diagrams and Carroll diagrams.*

- *Display a class birthday chart which includes the months of the year.*

- *Display and use a calendar.*

- *Have computer software related to mathematics available for use on the classroom computer(s) or in the computer room.*

- *Provide a range of measuring equipment for length, mass and capacity.*

- *Display the eight compass directions: N, S, E, W, NE, NW, SE, SW.*

- *Ensure you have a good selection of interactive maths resources for use on a whiteboard (refer to accompanying disk).*

Prim-Ed Publishing
www.prim-ed.com
Primary mathematics

Teachers notes

Measuring – Activities and games

- Use a geoboard to make shapes using different numbers of squares.

  Record the shapes made on either square dot paper or square grid paper.

  Check the perimeter and the area for each set of shapes made from the given number of squares. Write the perimeter and area on each shape; for example, a diagram of the shape on square dot paper, with area and perimeter marked.

- Select a variety of objects and order their mass by hefting. Each object should be compared by changing hands prior to making a decision. Repeat this activity a number of times using different objects.

- Pupils use balance scales (commercial or self-made) to compare and order the mass of a variety of self-chosen objects. Compare to see if larger objects are heavier.

- Pupils measure the mass of given objects against readily available materials; for example, sealed container of rice, nails, 2-cm cubes or other materials. Record results.

- Collect a variety of boxes, some the same size and some different. Fill the boxes with different materials so the boxes of the same size may have the same weight, or different; and the small boxes may be the same mass as larger boxes, heavier than them or lighter.

  Cover the boxes with self-adhesive plastic or something similar, so contents cannot be viewed or spilt. Label each box with either a number or a letter. Order the boxes by:

  (a) height   (b) length   (c) mass

  Record the order in sequence from smallest to greatest.

  Encourage pupils to talk and/or write about their discoveries.

- Pupils mark their birthdays and other important events onto a class calendar.

- Estimate and then check how long it takes to complete activities; for example, write out the five times table or run 100 metres.

Understanding shape – Activities and games

- Use an assortment of 2-D shapes to see which tessellate. Using a shape that tessellates, make a pattern to cover a page. Estimate how many shapes it will take to cover the page.

- Study various shapes and ask pupils to explain why some shapes will tile while others won't.

- Using a variety of 3-D shapes, classify them according to their attributes. Do the same with 2-D shapes. It may help to have headings on sheets of paper to assist in initial classification. Alternatively, use a Venn diagram.

- Using a local street map, instruct pupils to find the shortest path to school. Once marked on the map, direct pupils to find three different routes. Find the length of each route.

- Use three-dimensional shapes to see if a relationship between edges, faces and vertices can be determined. Results may be recorded on a table such as this.

Shape	Faces	Vertices	Edges
cube	6	8	12

- Make 3-D shapes from simple nets.

- (a) Make a cube using modelling clay.

  (b) Use fishing line to cut the cube of modelling clay to give the following cross-sectional shapes:

    – a square   – a rectangle

    – a triangle   – an equilateral triangle

    – a hexagon   – a regular hexagon

  (c) Is each cross-section congruent after the modelling clay is cut? How can pupils be sure?

  (d) Pupils trace around each cross-section and label it with the name of the shape made.

- Use pattern blocks to make simple patterns with one, two, three or four lines of symmetry. Record patterns and give to a classmate to find the line(s) of symmetry.

- Use the eight compass directions to locate places on a simple map.

Materials required

- *rulers/metre ruler*   • *containers of varying capacity*
- *trundle wheel*   • *balance scales*
- *grid paper*   • *bathroom scales*
- *calendar*   • *kitchen scales*
- *tape measure*   • *analogue and digital clocks*
- *simple timetables*   • *stop watch*

Materials required

- *2-D and 3-D shape pictures (see pages xii and xiii)*
- *2-D shapes for tessellation/symmetry*
- *construction material for 3-D models*
- *mirrors*   • *pattern blocks*
- *street map*   • *grid paper*
- *modelling clay/plasticine*
- *fishing line*

Year 4 Understanding shape – assessment checklist

Pupil's names	Draw polygons and classify them according to properties.	Classify polygons according to line symmetry.	Visualise 3-D objects from 2-D drawings.	Make nets of common solids.	Recognise horizontal and vertical lines.	Use the eight compass points.	Describe and identify the position of a square on a grid of squares.	Know that angles are measured in degrees.	Know that one whole turn is 360°.	Draw, compare and order angles less than 180°.

Key

D = Demonstrated
NFO = Needs further opportunity

Prim-Ed Publishing
www.prim-ed.com

Primary mathematics

Year 4 Measuring – assessment checklist

Key
D = Demonstrated
NFO = Needs further opportunity

Pupil's names	Use standard metric units and abbreviations of length.	Use standard metric units and abbreviations of weight.	Use standard metric units and abbreviations of capacity.	Know the meaning of kilo, centi and milli.	Use decimal notation to record measurements.	Interpret intervals and divisions on partially numbered scales.	Record readings accurately to the nearest tenth of a unit.	Measure the perimeter of rectangles.	Find the area of rectilinear shapes drawn on a square grid by counting the squares.	Read time to the nearest minute.	Use a.m., p.m. and 12-hour clock notation.	Choose units of time to measure time intervals.	Calculate time intervals from clocks and timetables.

Teacher resources

2-D shape flashcards

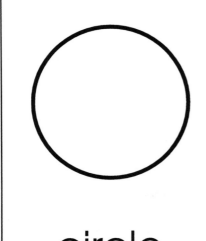

circle

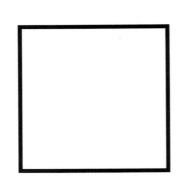

square

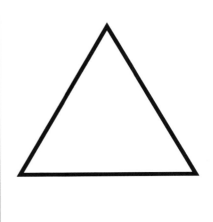

triangle

rectangle

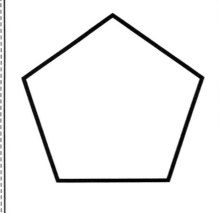

pentagon

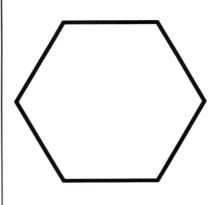

hexagon

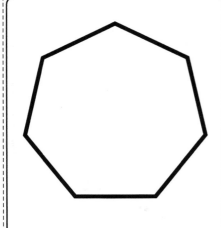

heptagon

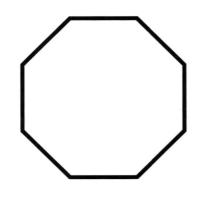

octagon

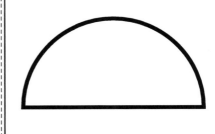

semicircle

Prim-Ed Publishing
www.prim-ed.com

Primary mathematics

sphere

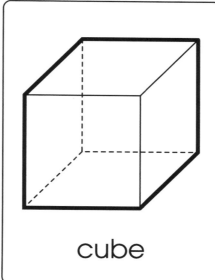

cube

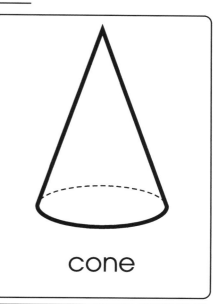

cone

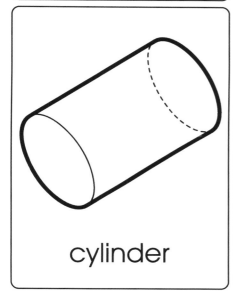

cylinder

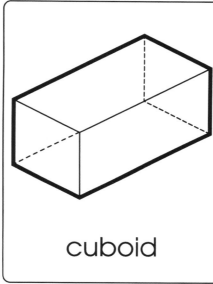

cuboid

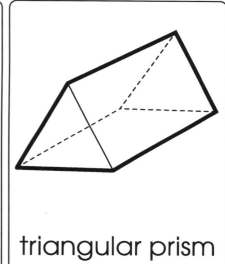

triangular prism

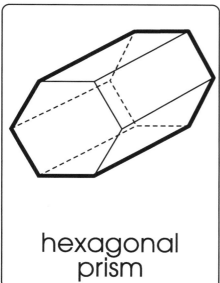

hexagonal prism

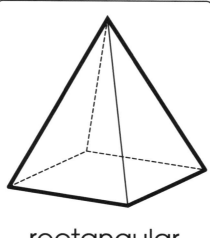

rectangular pyramid

triangular pyramid (tetrahedron)

Teacher resources

Eight compass directions

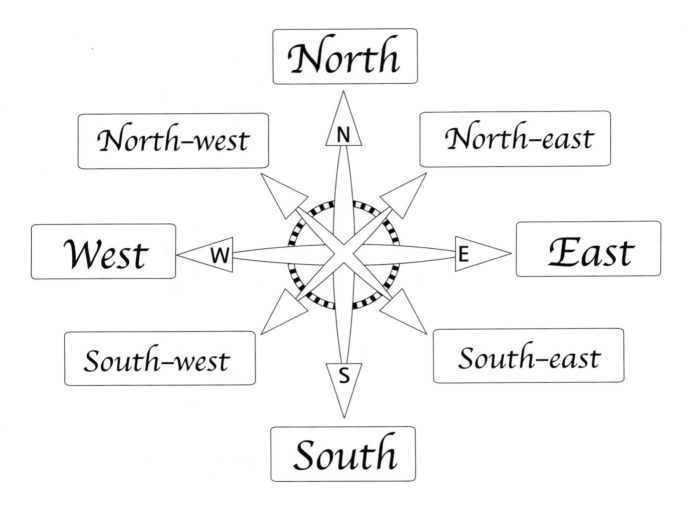

North

North-west

North-east

West

East

South-west

South-east

South

Teacher resources

Grids and co-ordinates

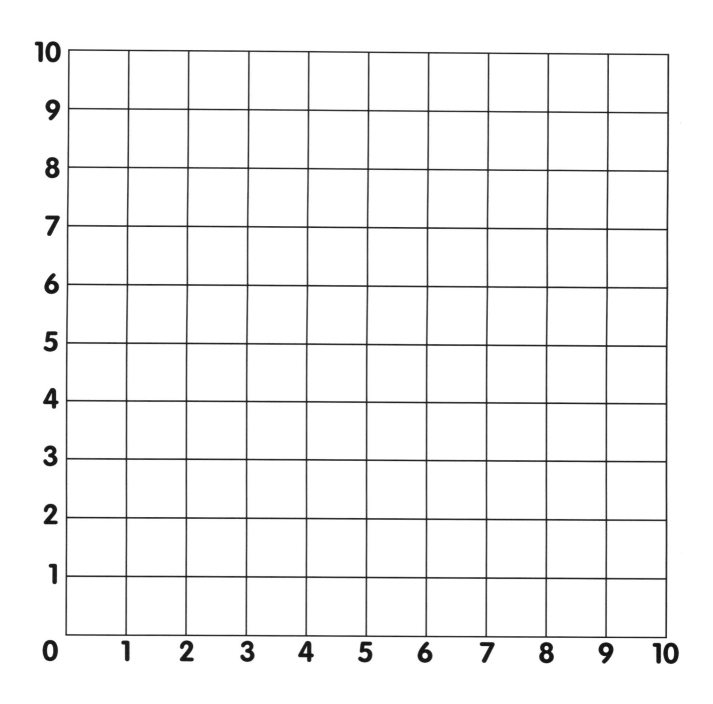

Teacher resources

Angles

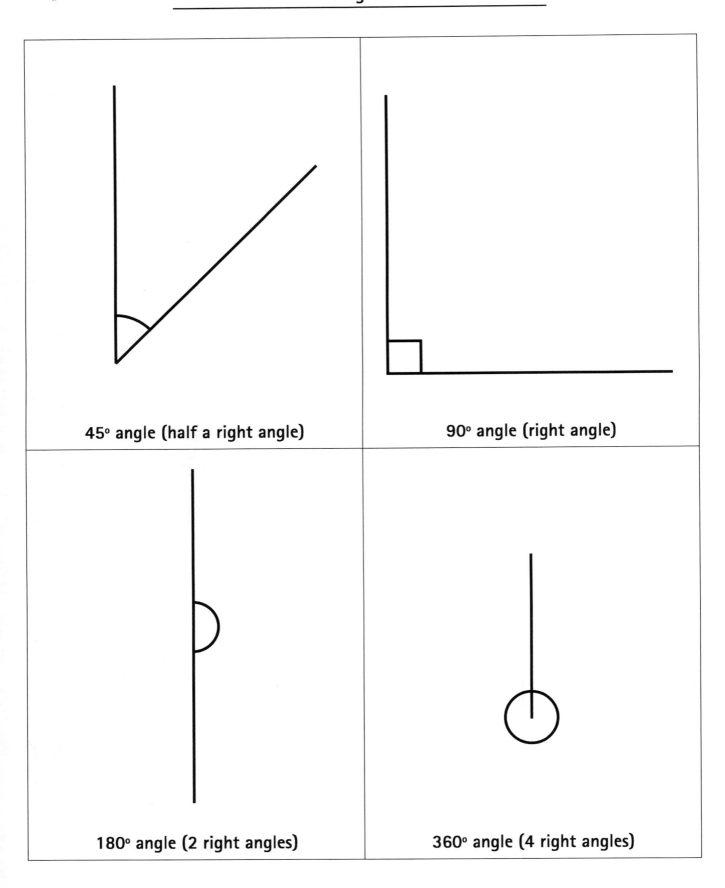

45° angle (half a right angle)

90° angle (right angle)

180° angle (2 right angles)

360° angle (4 right angles)

Prim–Ed Publishing
www.prim-ed.com

Primary mathematics

Teacher resources

Clock faces (blank)

TEACHER INFORMATION

UNDERSTANDING SHAPE

Objective
- Draw polygons and classify them by identifying their properties.

Oral work and mental calculation
- Use the correct names of 2-D shapes, including *pentagon, hexagon, heptagon, octagon, polygon, quadrilateral, equilateral triangle, isosceles triangle*.
- Use the vocabulary: *right angle, equal, curved, straight, side, corner*.
- Classify 2-D shapes in the classroom; for example, Who can see a shape that is a circle/hexagon/octagon?
- Play 'What am I?'. Teacher says a description of a 2-D shape and pupils have to name the shape; for example, I have three sides. Two of my angles are equal. What am I?
- Answer 'yes' or 'no' questions about a 2-D shape; for example, Does it have three equal sides? Does it have a curved side? Are all the sides equal lengths?

Main teaching activity
2-D shapes (page 3)

Additional activities suitable for developing the objective
- Sort 2-D shapes according to features; for example, the number of sides/corners or whether the sides are straight/curved.
- Play the 'feely-bag' game, where blindfolded pupils have to identify a 2-D shape in a bag, using the sense of touch only.
- Collect a range of triangles. Write a description for each one and then ask a partner to match each description to a triangle.
- Use different triangles as templates. Draw around them to make triangular patterns.
- Sort a set of 2-D shapes and display them on a Venn or Carroll diagram, according to their properties.

Answers
1. heptagon, triangle, octagon, square, pentagon, circle, hexagon, rectangle
2. All shapes, apart from the circle and oval should be coloured
3. (a) isosceles triangle: A triangle with two sides the same length and two angles the same size.
   (b) equilateral triangle: A triangle with three sides the same length and three angles the same size.

Challenge: Teacher check

1. Write the name of each shape.

circle, square, triangle, rectangle, pentagon, hexagon, heptagon, octagon

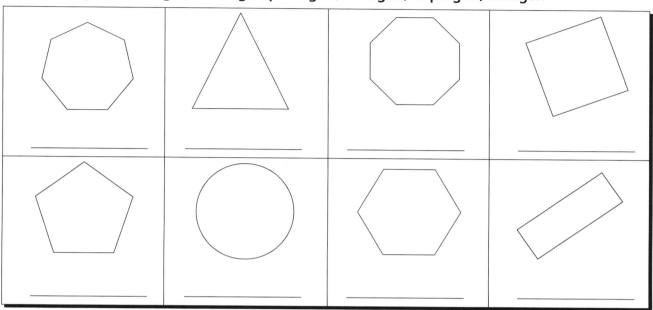

2. Polygons are shapes that are made up of three or more straight sides. Colour in the polygons only.

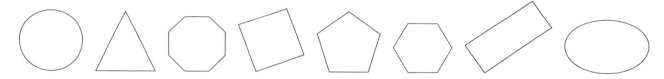

3. Triangles are shapes that are made up of three straight sides.
   Match each triangle to its name and description.

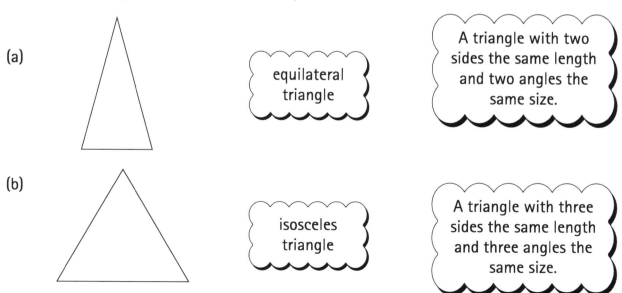

(a)

equilateral triangle

A triangle with two sides the same length and two angles the same size.

(b)

isosceles triangle

A triangle with three sides the same length and three angles the same size.

CHALLENGE On the back of the sheet, draw three different polygons using a ruler and name them.

UNDERSTANDING SHAPE

Objective
- Draw polygons and classify them by identifying their properties.

Oral work and mental calculation
- Use the correct names of 2-D shapes, including *pentagon, hexagon, heptagon, octagon, polygon, quadrilateral, equilateral triangle, isosceles triangle.*
- Use the vocabulary: *right angle, equal, curved, straight, side, corner.*
- Classify 2-D shapes in the classroom; for example, Who can see a shape that is a circle/hexagon/octagon?
- Play 'What am I?'. Teacher says a description of a 2-D shape and pupils have to name the shape; for example, I have three sides. Two of my angles are equal. What am I?
- Answer 'yes' or 'no' questions about a 2-D shape; for example, Does it have three equal sides? Does it have a curved side? Are all the sides equal lengths?

Main teaching activity
Describing 2-D shapes (page 5)

Additional activities suitable for developing the objective
- Sort 2-D shapes according to features; for example, the number of sides/corners or whether the sides are straight/curved.
- Play the 'feely-bag' game, where blindfolded pupils have to identify a 2-D shape in a bag, using the sense of touch only.
- Collect a range of triangles. Write a description for each one and then ask a partner to match each description to a triangle.
- Use different triangles as templates. Draw around them to make triangular patterns.
- Sort a set of 2-D shapes and display them on a Venn or Carroll diagram, according to their properties.

Answers
1. (a) hexagon, 6, 6　(b) square, 4, 4
   (c) circle, 1, 0　(d) pentagon, 5, 5
   (e) triangle, 3, 3　(f) heptagon, 7, 7
   (g) rectangle, 4, 4　(h) octagon, 8, 8

2. (a) equilateral triangle　(b) square
   (c) heptagon　(d) isosceles triangle
   (e) pentagon　(f) rectangle

Challenge: Teacher check

DESCRIBING 2-D SHAPES

1. Look at the shape, then fill in the description and shape name.

(a) name: _____ sides: _____ corners: _____	(b) name: _____ sides: _____ corners: _____
(c) name: _____ sides: _____ corners: _____	(d) name: _____ sides: _____ corners: _____
(e) name: _____ sides: _____ corners: _____	(f) name: _____ sides: _____ corners: _____
(g) name: _____ sides: _____ corners: _____	(h) name: _____ sides: _____ corners: _____

2. Read the description and name and draw the shape.

(a) a three-sided polygon with three angles the same size	(b) a quadrilateral with four equal sides and four right angles	(c) a polygon with seven equal sides
(d) a three-sided polygon with two sides the same length and one line of symmetry	(e) a polygon with five equal sides and five corners	(f) a quadrilateral with two short and two long sides and four right angles

CHALLENGE On the back of the sheet, make a list of all the different triangles you can see in the classroom.

UNDERSTANDING SHAPE

Objective

• Draw polygons and classify them by identifying their properties.

Oral work and mental calculation

• Look at 2-D shapes in a variety of fabric and wallpaper designs. Discuss the shapes used and how the pattern has been created.

• Identify 2-D shapes in the classroom; for example, the clock face is a circle, the maths book cover is a rectangle.

• Go for a walk around the school and look for shape patterns; for example, the rectangular tessellation of the bricks, the circular design on the staffroom curtains, the symmetry of the entrance door.

Main teaching activity

Tessellation (page 7)

Additional activities suitable for developing the objective

• Draw around a 2-D shape onto thin card. Cut it out and use it as a template to create a pattern.

• Use pattern blocks to create tessellating or symmetrical patterns.

• Investigate combining two shapes to create a different shape; for example, combining two squares will make a rectangle.

• Use a programmable robot to draw 2-D shapes.

• Continue patterns made up of 2-D shapes; for example, square, circle, triangle, square, circle, ..., ..., ...

• Use pinboards and elastic bands to make 2-D shapes. Describe the patterns and pictures made.

• Use plastic 2-D shapes as templates to draw pictures made up from 2-D shapes; for example, a house or a rocket.

• Construct 2-D shapes by paper folding. Look at the lines of symmetry on shapes created.

Answers

1. The following shapes should be coloured: triangles, rectangles, diamonds and squares.

2. Teacher check

Challenge: Teacher check

TESSELLATION

Tessellation is where shapes fit together to form a pattern without any gaps or overlapping.

1. Colour only the shapes that tessellate.

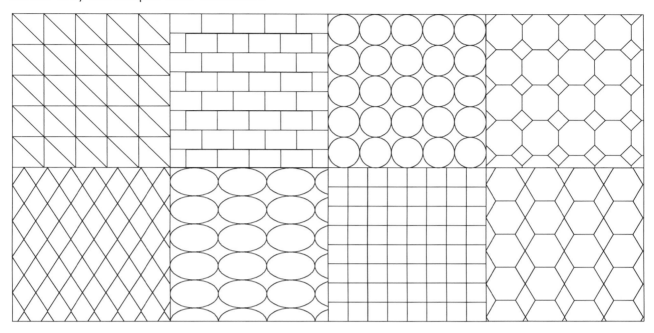

2. Continue these tessellating patterns.

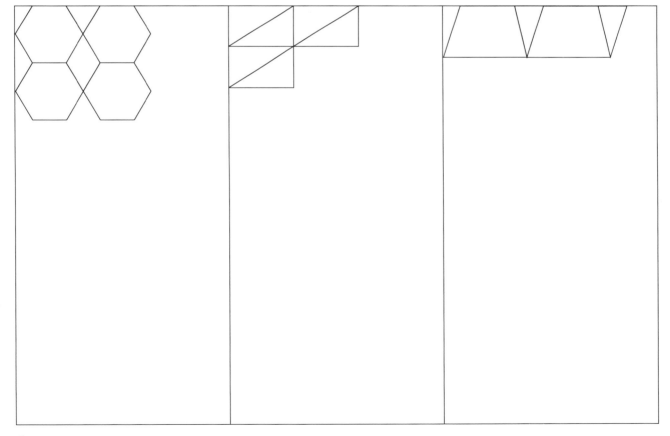

CHALLENGE On the back of the sheet, draw your own tessellating pattern and decorate it.

| Objective *Investigates and recognises tessellating shapes.* | **Primary mathematics** | Prim-Ed Publishing www.prim-ed.com | 7 |

TEACHER INFORMATION

UNDERSTANDING SHAPE

Objective
- Draw polygons and classify them by identifying their properties, including their line symmetry.

Oral work and mental calculation
- Use the vocabulary: *fold, line of symmetry, match, reflection, mirror line and symmetrical.*
- Look at and describe the symmetrical patterns in leaves, flowers, a cut apple, a butterfly etc.
- Look around the classroom to find examples of symmetrical objects.

Interactive whiteboard activity
Interactive whiteboard activity available to support this copymaster. See accompanying disk.

Main teaching activity
Lines of symmetry (page 9)

Additional activities suitable for developing the objective
- Sort a selection of 2-D shapes according to whether they have 0, 1, 2, 3, 4 or more than 4 lines of symmetry.
- Fold and cut paper to make symmetrical patterns.
- Write your name in capital letters. Draw the lines of symmetry onto the symmetrical letters.
- Look at a book of world flags. Draw a selection of flags that have line symmetry.
- Look through magazines to find examples of patterns, logos etc. with lines of symmetry.
- Complete a symmetrical pattern on a pegboard or squared graph paper.
- Sketch the reflection of a simple 2-D shape in a mirror line along one edge, using a mirror to help complete it.

Answers

1. (a)   (b)

   (c)  (d)

2. A B C D E F G H I J K L M N
   O P Q R S T U V W X Y Z

Challenge: Teacher check

LINES OF SYMMETRY

A line of symmetry or axis of symmetry is a line which divides a shape or object into two equal halves. The line may run in a number of directions depending on the shape.

For example:

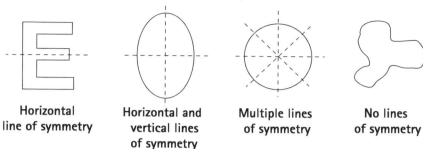

| Horizontal line of symmetry | Horizontal and vertical lines of symmetry | Multiple lines of symmetry | No lines of symmetry |

1. Use a ruler to draw lines of symmetry through these shapes. Remember, some shapes may need more than one line.

(a)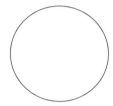

(b)

(c)

(d)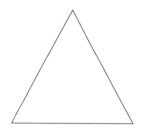

2. Draw lines through each letter of the alphabet. Some letters may need more than one line of symmetry. Some may have none.

A B C D E F G H I

J K L M N O P Q R

S T U V W X Y Z

CHALLENGE On the back of this sheet, draw a symmetrical face.

TEACHER INFORMATION

UNDERSTANDING SHAPE

Objective
- Draw polygons and classify them by identifying their properties, including their line symmetry.

Oral work and mental calculation
- Use the vocabulary: *fold, line of symmetry, match, reflection, mirror line* and *symmetrical*.
- Look at and describe the symmetrical patterns in leaves, flowers, a cut apple, a butterfly etc.
- Look around the classroom to find examples of symmetrical objects.

Main teaching activity
Symmetry (page 11)

Additional activities suitable for developing the objective
- Sort a selection of 2-D shapes according to whether they have 0, 1, 2, 3, 4 or more than 4 lines of symmetry.
- Fold and cut paper to make symmetrical patterns.
- Write your name in capital letters. Draw the lines of symmetry onto the symmetrical letters.
- Look at a book of world flags. Draw a selection of flags that have line symmetry.
- Look through magazines to find examples of patterns, logos etc. with lines of symmetry.
- Complete a symmetrical pattern on a pegboard or squared graph paper.
- Sketch the reflection of a simple 2-D shape in a mirror line along one edge, using a mirror to help complete it.

Answers
1. (a) equilateral triangle, 3
   (b) pentagon, 5 (c) octagon, 8
   (d) square, 4
2. Teacher check
3. Teacher check
Challenge: Teacher check

1. Name the shape, draw the line(s) of symmetry through each shape and record the number of lines of symmetry.

(a)	(b)	(c)	(d)
Name:	Name:	Name:	Name:
Lines:	Lines:	Lines:	Lines:

2. Complete the pictures, making them symmetrical.

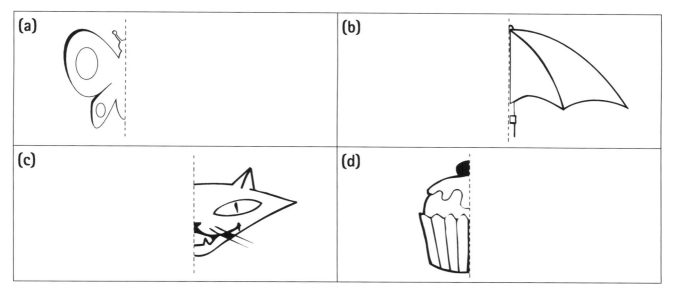

3. Copy this pattern, making it symmetrical.

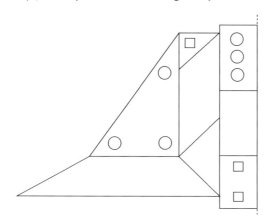

CHALLENGE Cut out a face from a magazine, then cut the face in half. Glue one half onto a sheet of paper and draw the other half, making it symmetrical.

UNDERSTANDING SHAPE

Objective
- Visualise 3-D objects from 2-D drawings.

Oral work and mental calculation
- Use the correct names of 3-D shapes, including *pyramid, prism, hemisphere and tetrahedron.*

- Extend vocabulary to include *right angled, equal, curved, vertex, vertices, pentagonal, hexagonal, heptagonal, octagonal.*

- Classify 3-D shapes in the classroom; for example, Who can see an object that is a cube? a sphere? a prism?

- Play 'What am I?'. Teacher says a description of a 3-D shape and pupils have to name the shape; for example, I have five faces, two of which are triangles and three of which are rectangles, what am I?

- Answer 'yes' or 'no' questions about a 3-D shape; for example, Does it have six faces? Are all the faces the same shape? Does it have five vertices?

Main teaching activity
3-D shapes (page 13)

Additional activities suitable for developing the objective
- Sort 3-D shapes according to features; for example, the number of faces/vertices/edges or whether the faces are straight/curved.

- Play the 'feely-bag' game, where blindfolded pupils have to identify a 3-D shape in a bag, using the sense of touch only.

- Collect a range of prisms. Write a description for each one and then ask a partner to match each description to a prism. Repeat activity for a range of pyramids.

- Sort a set of 3-D shapes and display them on a Venn or Carroll diagram, according to their properties.

- Collect objects that are common 3-D shapes, label them and create a display.

Answers
1. (a) sphere   (b) tetrahedron   (c) cube
   (d) cone   (e) cylinder
   (f) rectangular prism

2. cubes *(blue)*: Jack in the box
   cylinders *(red)*: Baked Beans, dog food
   prisms *(yellow)*: shoe box, Toblerone, loaf of bread, box of pencils
   pyramids *(green)*: chocolate pyramid

Challenge: Teacher check

3-D SHAPES

1. Write the shape name under the shape picture.

cube, cylinder, cone, sphere, rectangular prism, tetrahedron

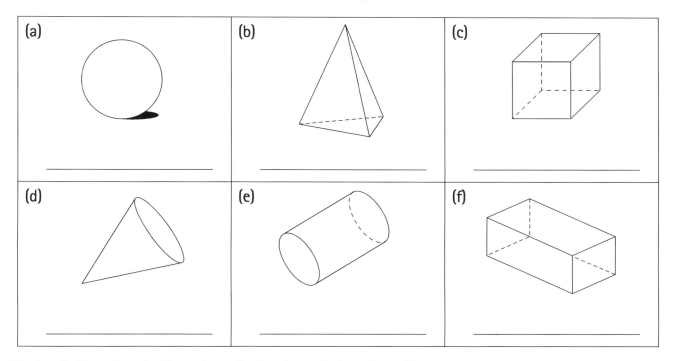

2. Circle all the cubes in blue, the cylinders in red, the prisms in yellow and the pyramids in green.

CHALLENGE On the back of the sheet, make a list of all the 3-D shapes you can see in the classroom.

UNDERSTANDING SHAPE

Objective

• Visualise 3-D objects from 2-D drawings.

Oral work and mental calculation

• Use the correct names of 3-D shapes, including *pyramid, prism, hemisphere and tetrahedron.*

• Extend vocabulary to include *right angled, equal, curved, vertex, vertices, pentagonal, hexagonal, heptagonal, octagonal.*

• Classify 3-D shapes in the classroom; for example, Who can see an object that is a cube? a sphere? a prism?

• Play 'What am I?'. Teacher says a description of a 3-D shape and pupils have to name the shape; for example, I have five faces, two of which are triangles and three of which are rectangles, what am I?

• Answer 'yes' or 'no' questions about a 3-D shape; for example, Does it have six faces? Are all the faces the same shape? Does it have five vertices?

Main teaching activity

Shape faces (page 15)

Additional activities suitable for developing the objective

• Sort 3-D shapes according to features; for example, the number of faces/vertices/edges or whether the faces are straight/curved.

• Play the 'feely-bag' game, where blindfolded pupils have to identify a 3-D shape in a bag, using the sense of touch only.

• Collect a range of prisms. Write a description for each one and then ask a partner to match each description to a prism. Repeat activity for a range of pyramids.

• Sort a set of 3-D shapes and display them on a Venn or Carroll diagram, according to their properties.

• Collect objects that are common 3-D shapes, label them and create a display.

Answers

1. (a) square   (b) triangle
   (c) circle, rectangle   (d) hexagon, rectangle
   (e) square, triangle   (f) triangle, rectangle

2. octagon, triangle

Challenge: Teacher check

SHAPE FACES

1. Colour the 2-D shapes that can be found on the faces of these 3-D shapes. In some cases there may be more than one shape.

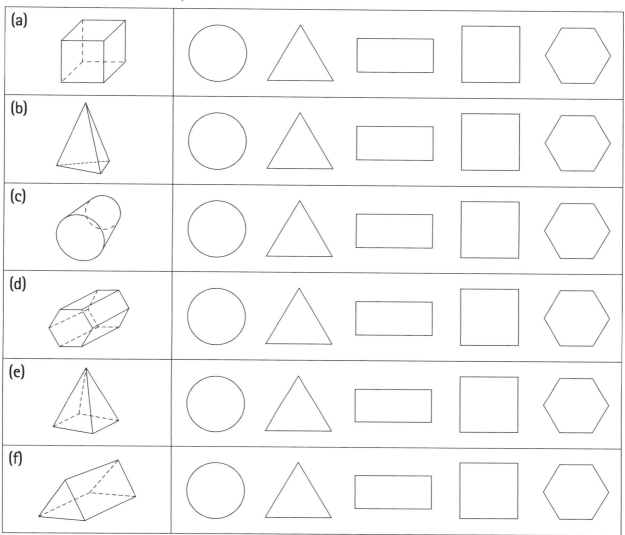

2. Draw and name the 2-D shapes you can see in this octagonal pyramid.

CHALLENGE Trace and cut out from cardboard two same-sized circles and one rectangle. Tape them together to make a cylinder.

Objective *Recognises 2-D faces within 3-D shapes.*   **Primary mathematics**   Prim-Ed Publishing www.prim-ed.com   **15**

UNDERSTANDING SHAPE

Objective
- Visualise 3-D objects from 2-D drawings.

Oral work and mental calculation
- Use the correct names of 3-D shapes, including *pyramid, prism, hemisphere* and *tetrahedron*.

- Extend vocabulary to include *right angled, equal, curved, vertex, vertices, pentagonal, hexagonal, heptagonal, octagonal*.

- Classify 3-D shapes in the classroom; for example, Who can see an object that is a cube? a sphere? a prism?

- Play 'What am I?'. Teacher says a description of a 3-D shape and pupils have to name the shape; for example, I have five faces, two of which are triangles and three of which are rectangles, what am I?

- Answer 'yes' or 'no' questions about a 3-D shape; for example, Does it have six faces? Are all the faces the same shape? Does it have five vertices?

Interactive whiteboard activity
Interactive whiteboard activity available to support this copymaster. See accompanying disk.

Main teaching activity
Describing 3-D shapes (page 17)

Additional activities suitable for developing the objective
- Sort 3-D shapes according to features; for example, the number of faces/vertices/edges or whether the faces are straight/curved.

- Play the 'feely-bag' game, where blindfolded pupils have to identify a 3-D shape in a bag, using the sense of touch only.

- Collect a range of prisms. Write a description for each one and then ask a partner to match each description to a prism. Repeat activity for a range of pyramids.

- Sort a set of 3-D shapes and display them on a Venn or Carroll diagram, according to their properties.

- Collect objects that are common 3-D shapes, label them and create a display.

Answers
1. (a) 6, 12, 8 (b) 1, 0, 0 (c) 3, 2, 0
   (d) 6, 12, 8 (e) 4, 6, 4 (f) 2, 1, 1

2. (a) hexagonal pyramid: 7 faces, 12 edges, 7 vertices
   (b) cube: 6 faces, 12 edges, 8 vertices
   (c) cylinder: 3 faces, 2 edges, 0 vertices

Challenge: Teacher check

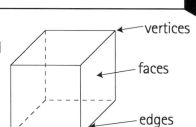

3-D shapes are described in terms of their faces, edges and vertices (corners).

1. Look at the shape and fill in the description.

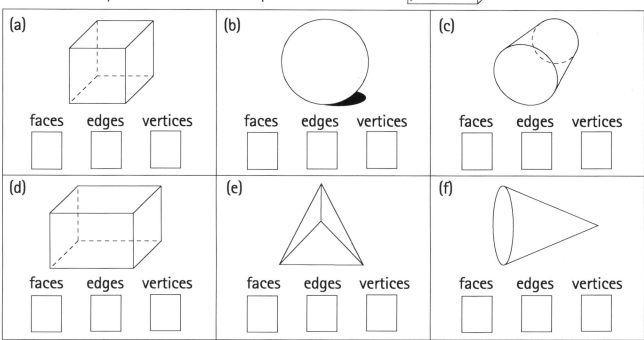

(a)

faces   edges   vertices

(b)

faces   edges   vertices

(c)

faces   edges   vertices

(d)

faces   edges   vertices

(e)

faces   edges   vertices

(f)

faces   edges   vertices

2. Draw lines to match the shape to its name and description.

(a)

(b)

(c)

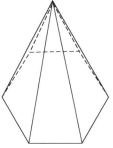
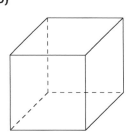
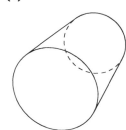

| Cube | Cylinder | Hexagonal Pyramid |

| 3 faces, 2 edges, 0 vertices | 7 faces, 12 edges, 7 vertices | 6 faces, 12 edges, 8 vertices |

CHALLENGE Draw and cut out from cardboard six same-sized squares, then tape them together to make a cube.

UNDERSTANDING SHAPE

Objective
- Visualise 3-D objects from 2-D drawings.

Oral work and mental calculation
- Use the correct names of 3-D shapes, including *pyramid, prism, hemisphere* and *tetrahedron*.

- Extend vocabulary to include *right angled, equal, curved, vertex, vertices, pentagonal, hexagonal, heptagonal, octagonal*.

- Classify 3-D shapes in the classroom; for example, Who can see an object that is a cube? a sphere? a prism?

- Play 'What am I?'. Teacher says a description of a 3-D shape and pupils have to name the shape; for example, I have five faces, two of which are triangles and three of which are rectangles, what am I?

- Answer 'yes' or 'no' questions about a 3-D shape; for example, Does it have six faces? Are all the faces the same shape? Does it have five vertices?

Main teaching activity
Prisms and pyramids (page 19)

Additional activities suitable for developing the objective
- Sort 3-D shapes according to features; for example, the number of faces/vertices/edges or whether the faces are straight/curved.

- Play the 'feely-bag' game, where blindfolded pupils have to identify a 3-D shape in a bag, using the sense of touch only.

- Collect a range of prisms. Write a description for each one and then ask a partner to match each description to a prism. Repeat activity for a range of pyramids.

- Cut cross-sections through prisms, to investigate the shapes of the cross-sections.

- Sort a set of 3-D shapes and display them on a Venn or Carroll diagram, according to their properties.

- Collect objects that are common 3-D shapes, label them and create a display.

Answers
1. (a) pentagonal prism   (b) octagonal prism
   (c) rectangular prism   (d) triangular prism
   (e) square prism   (f) hexagonal prism

2. (a) octagonal pyramid   (b) rectangular pyramid
   (c) pentagonal pyramid   (d) square pyramid
   (e) hexagonal pyramid   (f) triangular pyramid (tetrahedron)

Challenge: Teacher check

PRISMS AND PYRAMIDS

1. Prisms are named after their same shaped and sized ends, with all other faces being rectangles. Name these prisms.

rectangular prism, triangular prism, octagonal prism, pentagonal prism, hexagonal prism, square prism

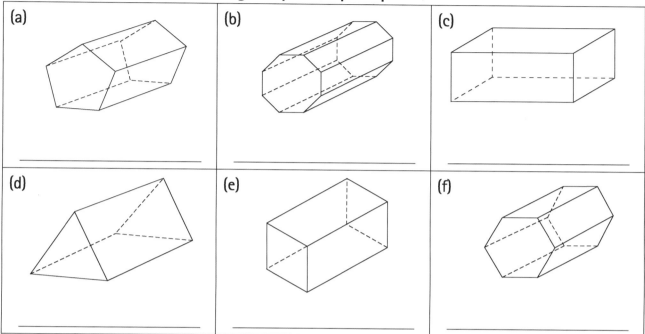

2. Pyramids are named after the shape of their base, with all the other faces being made up of triangles. Name these pyramids.

triangular pyramid (tetrahedron), square pyramid, rectangular pyramid, pentagonal pyramid, hexagonal pyramid, octagonal pyramid

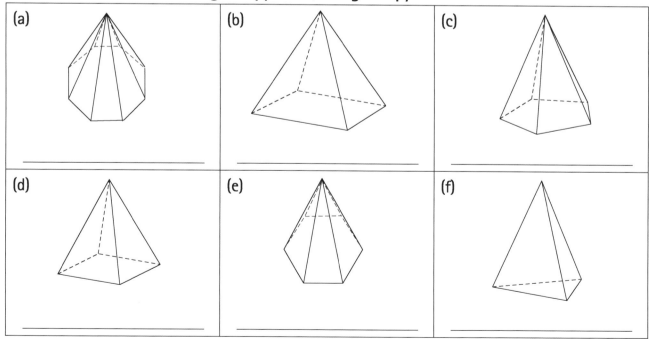

CHALLENGE On the back of this sheet, name three prisms and three pyramids you can see in the classroom.

UNDERSTANDING SHAPE

Objective

- Visualise 3-D objectives from 2-D drawings.

Oral work and mental calculation

- Identify 3-D shapes in the classroom; for example, the box of tissues is a cube, the football is a sphere.

- Go for a walk around the school and identify 3-D shapes in the environment; for example, the rubbish bins are cylinders, the roof on the games shed is a triangular prism.

Main teaching activity

3-D models (page 21)

Additional activities suitable for developing the objective

- Write a list of everyday objects that are common 3-D shapes; for example, a toilet roll, can of peas and tube of Smarties are all cylinders.

- Look through magazines and make a collection of all the 3-D shapes that pupils can find in advertisements.

- Use construction kits to build models of 3-D shapes. Count the number of faces, edges and vertices.

- Use plastic or wooden 3-D shapes to construct a model of a house/spaceship. Keep a record of which shapes were used for each part of the model.

- Investigate the different 3-D shapes that can be made by joining four interlocking cubes. Which pupil can find the most different shapes?

- Make 3-D shapes using straws or pipe cleaners. Make a mobile of 3-D shapes to hang from the ceiling.

Answers

1. Teacher check models made.

    (a) rectangular pyramid, 8
    (b) square prism, 12
    (c) pentagonal prism, 15
    (d) cube, 12
    (e) tetrahedron, 6
    (f) hexagonal prism, 18

2. Teacher check models made.

    (a) cube   (b) cylinder   (c) sphere

Challenge: Teacher check

3-D MODELS

1. Name these shapes. Use straws (you may need to cut some in half) and modelling clay to make these prism and pyramid models. Record the number of lengths you used.

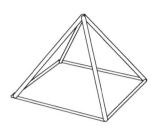
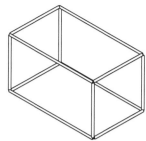
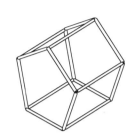

| (a)   Rectangular
Pyramid

8 lengths | (b)

_____ lengths | (c)

_____ lengths |

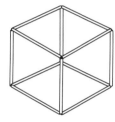
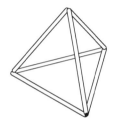
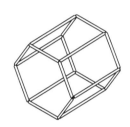

| (d)

_____ lengths | (e)

_____ lengths | (f)

_____ lengths |

2. Name these shapes. Make models of these shapes using modelling clay.

(a)

(b)

(c)

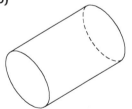

_____   _____   _____

CHALLENGE Using matchsticks and modelling clay, make models of your own choice. Show a friend.

Objective *Identifies and constructs simple 3-D models.*   **Primary mathematics**   Prim-Ed Publishing
www.prim-ed.com   **21**

UNDERSTANDING SHAPE

Objectives
- Visualise 3-D objects from 2-D drawings.
- Make nets of common solids.

Oral work and mental calculation
- Identify 3-D shapes in the classroom; for example, the box of tissues is a cube, the football is a sphere.
- Go for a walk around the school and identify 3-D shapes in the environment; for example, the rubbish bins are cylinders, the roof on the games shed is a triangular prism.
- Look at cardboard boxes; for example, cubes (tissue box), cuboids (cereal box), cylinders (tube of Smarties), and more unusual shaped boxes; for example, triangular prisms (Toblerone box). Unfold each box and look at the net.

Interactive whiteboard activity
Interactive whiteboard activity available to support this copymaster. See accompanying disk.

Main teaching activity
Shape nets (page 23)

Additional activities suitable for developing the objectives
- Write a list of everyday objects that are common 3-D shapes; for example, a toilet roll, can of peas and tube of Smarties are all cylinders.
- Look through magazines and make a collection of all the 3-D shapes that pupils can find in advertisements.
- Use construction kits to build models of 3-D shapes. Count the number of faces, edges and vertices.
- Use plastic or wooden 3-D shapes to construct a model of a house/spaceship. Keep a record of which shapes were used for each part of the model.
- Investigate the different 3-D shapes that can be made by joining four interlocking cubes. Which pupil can find the most different shapes?
- Make 3-D shapes using straws or pipe cleaners. Make a mobile of 3-D shapes to hang from the ceiling.
- Cut out, fold and glue together simple given nets to make 3-D shapes.
- Use squared paper to draw and make a net of a cube.

Answers
1. Teacher check

2. (a) cube   (b) cone
   (c) triangular prism   (d) octagonal pyramid

3. Teacher check; hexagonal prism

Challenge: (a) 5 (b) 6 (c) 8

SHAPE NETS

1. Match the 3-D shape to its net by colouring them the same colour.

(a)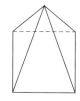

(b)

(c)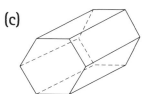

(d)

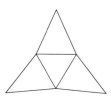

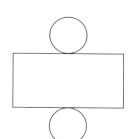

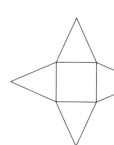

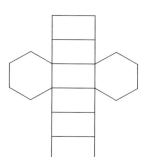

2. Write the name of the shape under its net.

(a)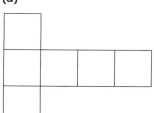

(b)

(c)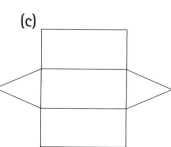

(d)

_____   _____   _____   _____

_____   _____   _____   _____

3. Cut out this net and glue it together. Write the name of the shape on it.

CHALLENGE How many triangles would you find on a

(a) pentagonal pyramid net? _____

(b) hexagonal pyramid net? _____

(c) octagonal pyramid net? _____

TEACHER INFORMATION

UNDERSTANDING SHAPE

Objective
- Recognise horizontal and vertical lines.

Oral work and mental calculation
- Use the vocabulary: *line, horizontal, vertical, straight, curved, wavy, zig-zagged, parallel, diagonal.*
- Discuss the word 'horizon', what it means and how this relates to the word 'horizontal'.
- Look for and list examples of horizontal and vertical lines in the classroom.
- Go for a 'Line trail' walk around the school to identify examples of horizontal and vertical lines – both inside and outside.

Interactive whiteboard activity
Interactive whiteboard activity available to support this copymaster. See accompanying disk.

Main teaching activity
Lines (page 25)

Additional activities suitable for developing the objective
- Draw examples of different types of lines; for example, horizontal, vertical, straight, curved, wavy, zig-zagged, parallel, diagonal.
- Sort pictures of objects according to whether they have horizontal or vertical lines.
- Draw objects that have horizontal and vertical lines.
- Complete a Venn diagram to sort objects with horizontal and vertical lines.
- Draw a picture of a house/boat/castle/robot using some horizontal and vertical lines. Draw over the horizontal lines in red and the vertical lines in blue.

Answers
1. Teacher check
2. (a) vertical (b) diagonal (c) parallel
   (d) horizontal (e) wavy (f) zig-zagged
3. Teacher check

Challenge: Teacher check

1. Draw an example of each line type under the headings.

   (a) straight   (b) curved   (c) wavy   (d) zig-zagged

   (e) parallel lines   (f) vertical   (g) horizontal   (h) diagonal

2. Write the correct words under the pictures.

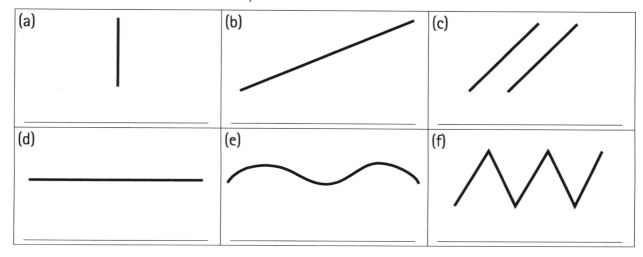

3. In the picture below, trace over all the horizontal lines in red, the vertical lines in blue and the diagonal lines in yellow.

CHALLENGE On the back of this sheet, draw a house made up of horizontal, vertical and diagonal lines. Add a wavy garden path to the front door.

UNDERSTANDING SHAPE

Objective

- Use the eight compass points to describe direction.

Oral work and mental calculation

- Use a compass to discover which way is north, south, east and west.

- Call out north, south, east or west. Pupils jump to face the correct direction.

- Say/Chant silly rhymes; for example, 'Naughty elephants squirt water', to help aid memory of the order of the compass points.

- Extend to the eight compass points. Explain how NE is named because it is halfway between N and E, and so on.

- Use an overhead projector or whiteboard with a grid on it. Move a counter up (N), down (S), left (W), right (E), diagonally up/left (NW), diagonally up/right (NE), diagonally down/left (SW) and diagonally down/right (SE).

- Follow verbal instructions on the above grid; for example, move the counter north for three squares, west for 2 squares and south-east for four squares. Where are you?

Interactive whiteboard activity

Interactive whiteboard activity available to support this copymaster. See accompanying disk.

Main teaching activity

Compass points (page 27)

Additional activities suitable for developing the objective

- Use squared paper and a counter to move; for example, from A3 to D5, describing the route as three squares east and two squares north.

- Give instructions to a programmable robot, to navigate a route.

- Draw a map of an imaginary place. Write a list to show what can be found in eight compass points of the place.

- Look at a map of Britain or the world. Name places that are found in the north, south, east, west, north-east, north-west, south-east and south-west.

Answers

1.-2.

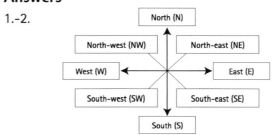

3. (a) N   (b) SE   (c) SW   (d) NE
    (e) W   (f) N   (g) S   (h) SW

Challenge: Teacher check

1. If you know the direction of north it is easier to find south, east and west. Fill in the three other major points of the compass first.

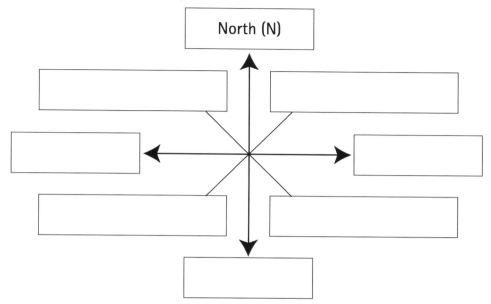

North (N)

2. To make directions more accurate there are other compass points in between the four main ones. These include north-east (NE), south-east (SE), north-west (NW) and south-west (SW). Place these on the compass above.

3. Look at the map of the aquarium and use the compass above to answer the questions.

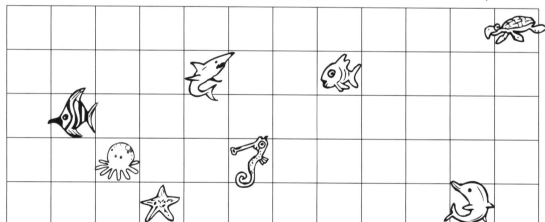

In what direction is the...

(a) shark? _____

(b) dolphin? _____

(c) octopus? _____

(d) turtle? _____

(e) tropical fish? _____

(f) goldfish? _____

(g) sea horse? _____

(h) starfish? _____

CHALLENGE In the classroom, name something you will find in the NE, NW, SE and SW.

UNDERSTANDING SHAPE

Objective

- Use the eight compass points to describe direction.

Oral work and mental calculation

- Use a compass to discover which way is north, south, east and west.

- Call out north, south, east or west. Pupils jump to face the correct direction.

- Say/Chant silly rhymes; for example, 'Naughty elephants squirt water', to help aid memory of the order of the compass points.

- Extend to the eight compass points. Explain how NE is named because it is halfway between N and E, and so on.

- Use an overhead projector or whiteboard with a grid on it. Move a counter up (N), down (S), left (W), right (E), diagonally up/left (NW), diagonally up/right (NE), diagonally down/left (SW) and diagonally down/right (SE).

- Follow verbal instructions on the above grid; for example, move the counter north for three squares, west for 2 squares and south-east for four squares. Where are you?

Main teaching activity

Compass directions (page 29)

Additional activities suitable for developing the objective

- Use squared paper and a counter to move; for example, from A3 to D5, describing the route as three squares east and two squares north.

- Give instructions to a programmable robot, to navigate a route.

- Draw a map of an imaginary place. Write a list to show what can be found in eight compass points of the place.

- Look at a map of Britain or the world. Name places that are found in the north, south, east, west, north-east, north-west, south-east and south-west.

Answers

1. (a) N   (b) E   (c) W   (d) SW
(e) crocodile (f) penguin   (g) dolphin   (h) shark

2. Teacher check

Challenge: Teacher check

COMPASS DIRECTIONS

1. Look at the map of the classroom below and fill in the missing words in the sentences.

(a) The teacher's desk is to the

_____ of the classroom.

(b) The door and the corridor are to the

_____ of the classroom.

(c) The display board is to the

_____ of the classroom.

(d) The filing cabinet and sports equipment

are to the _____.

(e) To the west of the dolphin

group is the

_____ group.

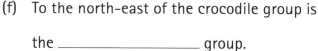

(f) To the north-east of the crocodile group is

the _____ group.

(g) The _____ group is
south-east of the stingray group.

(h) The _____ group is
north-west of the penguin group.

2. Start at the cross and follow the directions, colouring the squares as you go.

Move west 2 squares.

Move north 4 squares.

Move south-east 5 squares.

Move south 2 squares.

Move north-west 2 squares.

Move south-west 3 squares.

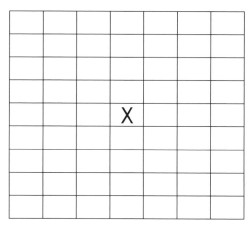

CHALLENGE On the back of the sheet, design your own ideal classroom set up. Include all the things you would like to see in a classroom.

UNDERSTANDING SHAPE

Objective

- Describe and identify the position of a square on a grid of squares.

Oral work and mental calculation

- Use the vocabulary: *grid, row, column, coordinates, map, plan.*

- Explain how coordinates work and are found. Ensure pupils know that to read or plot coordinates they need to go along the horizontal axis first and then up the vertical axis. Help them to remember this by using the phrase 'go along the corridor and up the stairs'. Ensure that pupils realise that coordinates (3,2) and (2,3) are not the same and that each gives a different position.

- Play a class game of 'Noughts and crosses' on the whiteboard, using a grid and grid references.

- Draw a grid on the whiteboard. Encourage pupils to come and draw 2-D shapes on given grid references.

- Join given coordinates to create a picture.

Interactive whiteboard activity

Interactive whiteboard activity available to support this copymaster. See accompanying disk.

Main teaching activity

Map keys – 1 (page 31)

Additional activities suitable for developing the objective

- Play 'Battleships' with a partner.

- Draw a map of a treasure island onto a grid. Write instructions to find the treasure, using grid references.

- Give instructions to a programmable robot, to get to a certain point on a grid.

- Position the desks in the classroom to form a grid. Make a plan to show which pupil sits where and write the coordinates for each pupil.

- Join given coordinates to create a picture.

Answers

1. (a) forest   (b) mountains
   (c) lake   (d) (5,4)
   (e) (8,2) or (3,3)   (f) (6,4), (7,4) and (8,4)

2. Teacher check

Challenge: Teacher check

A map key gives you information about what can be found on a map. Symbols are used to represent main features, which are then in turn included on the key.

1. Look at the map and the key to answer the questions.

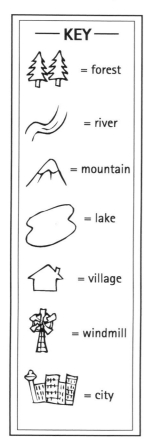

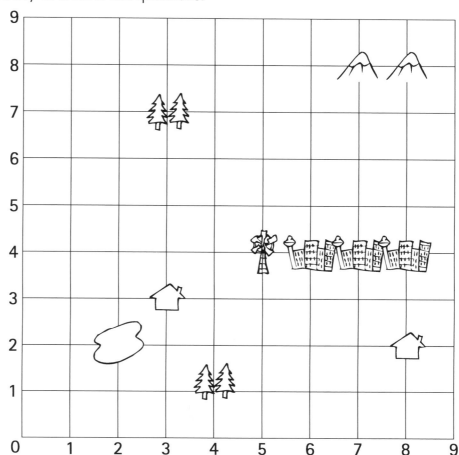

(a) What will you find at (4,1) and (3,7)? _____

(b) What will you find at (7,8) and (8,8)? _____

(c) What will you find at (2,2)? _____

(d) Where will you find a windmill? _____

(e) Where will you find a village? _____

(f) Where will you find the city? _____

2. On the map above, draw...

(a) a forest at (6,3)

(b) A village in (4,6)

(c) a river running through (1,7) and (2,8)

 CHALLENGE On the back of the sheet, draw your own key to represent things you will find at a local shopping centre.

UNDERSTANDING SHAPE

Objective
• Describe and identify the position of a square on a grid of squares.

Oral work and mental calculation
• Use the vocabulary: *grid, row, column, coordinates, map, plan.*

• Explain how coordinates work and are found. Ensure pupils know that to read or plot coordinates they need to go along the horizontal axis first and then up the vertical axis. Help them to remember this by using the phrase 'go along the corridor and up the stairs'. Ensure that pupils realise that coordinates (3,2) and (2,3) are not the same and that each gives a different position.

• Play a class game of 'Noughts and crosses' on the whiteboard, using a grid and grid references.

• Draw a grid on the whiteboard. Encourage pupils to come and draw 2-D shapes on given grid references.

• Join given coordinates to create a picture.

Main teaching activity
Map keys – 2 (page 33)

Additional activities suitable for developing the objective
• Play 'Battleships' with a partner.

• Draw a map of a treasure island onto a grid. Write instructions to find the treasure, using grid references.

• Give instructions to a programmable robot, to get to a certain point on a grid.

• Position the desks in the classroom to form a grid. Make a plan to show which pupil sits where and write the coordinates for each pupil.

• Join given coordinates to create a picture.

Answers
1. (a) deli   (b) school   (c) park and fountain
    (d) car park   (e) (4,6)   (f) (3,8)
    (g) (6,4)   (h) (2,3)

2. Teacher check

Challenge: Teacher check

1. Look at this town grid map and use the letter and number coordinates to help you answer the questions below.

KEY

	bakery		petrol station
	deli		car park
	chemist		supermarket
	newsagency		hospital
	post office		vet
	train station		school
	public toilets		park and fountain

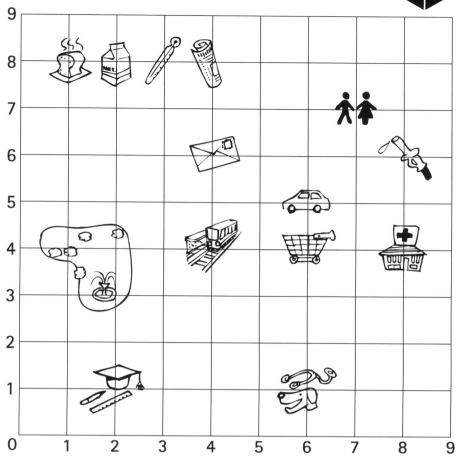

(a) What will you find at (2,8)?

_____

(b) What will you find at (2,1)?

_____

(c) What will you find at (1,4) and (2,4)?

_____

(d) What will you find at (6,5)?

_____

(e) Where will you find the post office?

_____

(f) Where will you find the chemist?

_____

(g) Where will you find the supermarket?

_____

(h) Where will you find the fountain?

_____

2. Draw these things on the town map.

(a) A lake across (4, 2) and (5, 2).

(b) A red cross to represent a doctor's surgery in (8, 3).

(c) A coffee cup to represent a cafe in (2, 7).   (d) A bus stop sign in (4, 5).

CHALLENGE Use grid paper labelled with coordinates to play a game of 'Battleships' with a classmate.

UNDERSTANDING SHAPE

Objective

- Know that angles are measured in degrees and that one whole turn is 360°.

Oral work and mental calculation

- Use the vocabulary: *clockwise, anticlockwise, right angle, 90°, 180°, 360°, quarter turn, half turn, whole turn, degree.*

- Follow instructions; for example, Face north and turn clockwise through one right angle or 90°. Which direction are you facing?

- Look at a large-format analogue clock. Turn the big hand in different directions; for example, anticlockwise for 180°.

- Look for right angles and straight line angles in the classroom.

- Use geo-strips to demonstrate right angles and straight line angles.

Interactive whiteboard activity

Interactive whiteboard activity available to support this copymaster. See accompanying disk.

Main teaching activity

Clockwise and anticlockwise (page 35)

Additional activities suitable for developing the objective

- Sort 2-D shapes according to whether they have right angles.

- Fold a piece of paper to make a right angle. Use it to find right angles in the classroom. Write a list of right angles found.

- Draw and label classroom objects that have right angles.

- Make and describe 30°, 60° and 90° turns, using the hour hand on a clock face.

- Answer word problems; for example, The ship was sailing south. A strong wind turned it 90° clockwise. What direction was it now sailing?

Answers

1. (a) Teacher check   (b) Teacher check
   (c) Teacher check   (d) Teacher check
   (e) Teacher check, quarter, 90, 1
   (f) Teacher check, half, 180, 2
   (g) Teacher check, quarter, 90, 3
   (h) Teacher check, whole, 360, 4
   (i) Teacher check, quarter, 90, 1
   (j) Teacher check, half, 180, 2

Challenge: (a) South (b) West

CLOCKWISE AND ANTICLOCKWISE

Clockwise means in the same direction as the movement of the hands of a clock.	Anticlockwise means in the opposite direction as the movement of the hands of a clock.
 clockwise	 anticlockwise

1. Move the big hand on the clock faces in the correct direction.

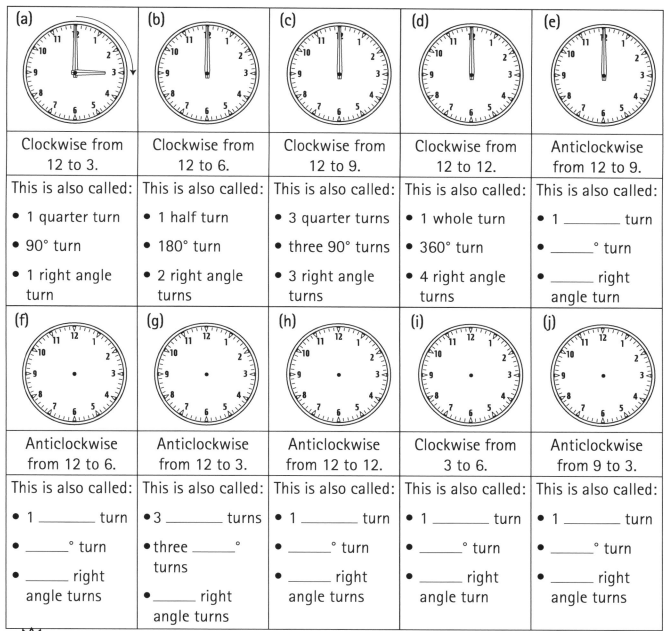

(a)	(b)	(c)	(d)	(e)
Clockwise from 12 to 3.	Clockwise from 12 to 6.	Clockwise from 12 to 9.	Clockwise from 12 to 12.	Anticlockwise from 12 to 9.
This is also called:	This is also called:	This is also called:	This is also called:	This is also called:
• 1 quarter turn • 90° turn • 1 right angle turn	• 1 half turn • 180° turn • 2 right angle turns	• 3 quarter turns • three 90° turns • 3 right angle turns	• 1 whole turn • 360° turn • 4 right angle turns	• 1 _____ turn • _____° turn • _____ right angle turn
(f)	(g)	(h)	(i)	(j)
Anticlockwise from 12 to 6.	Anticlockwise from 12 to 3.	Anticlockwise from 12 to 12.	Clockwise from 3 to 6.	Anticlockwise from 9 to 3.
This is also called:	This is also called:	This is also called:	This is also called:	This is also called:
• 1 _____ turn • _____° turn • _____ right angle turns	• 3 _____ turns • three _____° turns • _____ right angle turns	• 1 _____ turn • _____° turn • _____ right angle turns	• 1 _____ turn • _____° turn • _____ right angle turn	• 1 _____ turn • _____° turn • _____ right angle turns

CHALLENGE Face north. On the back of the sheet, complete the turns to see which direction you are facing after: (a) 1 half turn clockwise (b) 1 quarter turn anticlockwise

UNDERSTANDING SHAPE

Objective

- Compare angles less than 180º.

Oral work and mental calculation

- Use the vocabulary: *right angle, 90˚, 180˚, 360˚, quarter turn, half turn, whole turn, degree.*
- Look for right angles, half right angles and straight line angles in the classroom.
- Use geo-strips to demonstrate right angles and straight line angles.

Main teaching activity

Angles (page 37)

Additional activities suitable for developing the objective

- Sort 2-D shapes according to whether they have right angles.
- Fold a piece of paper to make a right angle. Use it to find right angles in the classroom. Write a list of right angles found.
- Use two geo-strips to make right angles, straight line angles, angles smaller than a right angle and angles greater than a right angle.
- Look at an assortment of angles. Sort them into two groups; angles which are smaller than a right angle and angles which are larger.
- Draw and label classroom objects that have right angles.
- Use a set square to draw angles of 45˚ and 90˚.

Answers

1. Teacher check
2. Right angles *(red)* = a, c, d and g
   Straight line angles *(yellow)* = b and h
   Half right angles *(blue)* = e, f and i

Challenge: Square or rectangle.

Angles can be found everywhere, especially right angles, which are the most common. When a horizontal and vertical line join (perpendicular lines) they form a right angle at the corner.

1. Find and draw three right angles in the classroom.

(a)	(b)	(c)

A right angle is 90°. A straight angle (two right angles) is 180°.
Half a right angle is 45°.

2. Trace over the right angles in red. Trace the straight line angles in yellow and the half-right angles in blue.

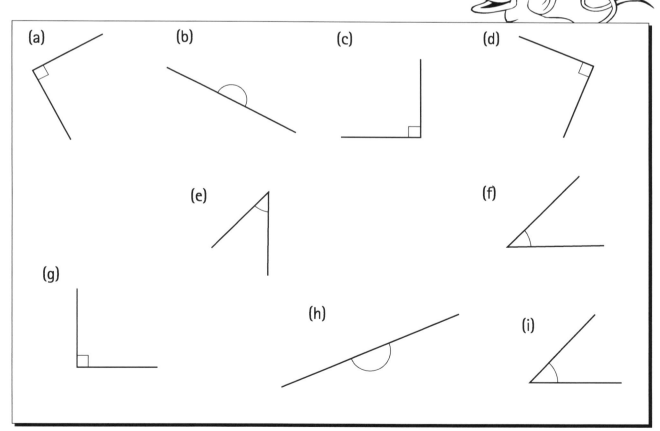

CHALLENGE On the back of this sheet, draw and write the name of a shape that has four right angles.

UNDERSTANDING SHAPE

Objective
- Compare angles less than 180º.

Oral work and mental calculation
- Use the vocabulary: *right angle, 90˚, 180˚, 360˚, quarter turn, half turn, whole turn, degree.*
- Look for right angles, half right angles and straight line angles in the classroom.
- Use geo-strips to demonstrate right angles and straight line angles.

Main teaching activity
Identifying angles (page 39)

Additional activities suitable for developing the objective
- Sort 2-D shapes according to whether they have right angles.
- Fold a piece of paper to make a right angle. Use it to find right angles in the classroom. Write a list of right angles found.
- Use two geo-strips to make right angles, straight line angles, angles smaller than a right angle and angles greater than a right angle.
- Look at an assortment of angles. Sort them into two groups; angles which are smaller than a right angle and angles which are larger.
- Draw and label classroom objects that have right angles.
- Use a set square to draw angles of 45˚ and 90˚.

Answers
1. Teacher check
2. The following shapes should be coloured red: a, c, e, g and h.

Challenge: Teacher check

An angle can be found where two lines meet.

The right angle (90°) is the most common angle found. ⌐

The 180° angle is also common. ⌒

The 45° angle is half a right angle. ∠

Angles are measured by the amount of space between the lines.

1. Look at the picture below and locate these angles.

   (a) Trace over the right angles in red.

   (b) Trace over the 45° angles in blue.

   (c) Trace over the 180° angles in green.

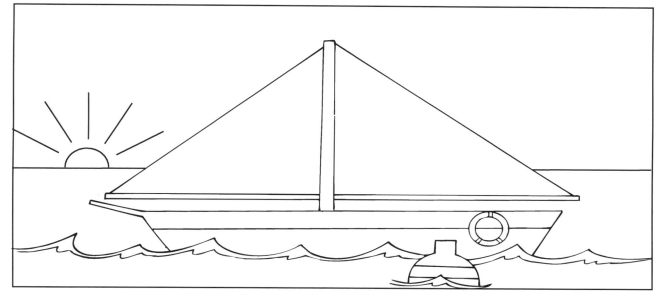

2. Colour the shapes with right angles red.

(a)    (b)   (c)    (d)

(e)   (f) 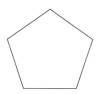   (g)    (h)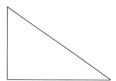

CHALLENGE List the 180° angles you can see in the classroom.

UNDERSTANDING SHAPE

Objective

- Compare and order angles less than 180°.

Oral work and mental calculation

- Use the vocabulary: *right angle, 90°, 180°, 360°, quarter turn, half turn, whole turn, degree.*

- Look for right angles, half right angles and straight line angles in the classroom.

- Use geo-strips to demonstrate right angles and straight line angles.

- Sort a selection of angles from smallest to largest, and vice versa.

Interactive whiteboard activity

Interactive whiteboard activity available to support this copymaster. See accompanying disk.

Main teaching activity

Ordering angles (page 41)

Additional activities suitable for developing the objective

- Sort 2-D shapes according to whether they have right angles.

- Fold a piece of paper to make a right angle. Use it to find right angles in the classroom. Write a list of right angles found.

- Use two geo-strips to make right angles, straight line angles, angles smaller than a right angle and angles greater than a right angle.

- Look at an assortment of angles. Sort them into two groups; angles which are smaller than a right angle and angles which are larger.

- Draw and label classroom objects that have right angles.

- Use a set square to draw angles of 45° and 90°.

- Sort a selection of drawn angles from smallest to largest, and vice versa.

- Write a list of angles in order from smallest to largest, and vice versa; for example, 20°, 45°, 90°, 180°.

Answers

1. (a) 45°   (b) 90°   (c) 180°

2. (a) 1   (b) 4   (c) 3   (d) 2

3. (a) 4   (b) 1   (c) 2   (d) 3

Challenge: Teacher check

1. Make these angles using lolly sticks and label them correctly: 45°, 90°, 180°.
   Tick when you have completed each model.

   (a) completed ☐   (b) completed ☐   (c) completed ☐

A line that has travelled in a complete circle has a 360° angle.

2. Order these angles from the smallest (1) to the largest (4).

   (a)   (b)   (c)   (d)

3. Order these angles from the largest (1) to the smallest (4).

   (a)   (b)   (c)   (d)

        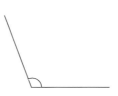   

☐   ☐   ☐   ☐

 Write the names of two shapes that have ...

   (a) right angles _____ and _____

   (b) angles smaller than right angles _____ and _____

   (c) angles larger than right angles _____ and _____

MEASURING

Objectives

- Choose and use standard metric units and their abbreviations.
- Use decimal notation to record measurements.

Oral work and mental calculation

- Use the vocabulary: *millimetre, centimetre, metre, kilometre, mile.*
- Ask verbal equivalence questions; for example, 10 millimetres is the same as how many centimetres? $^3/_4$ of 1 kilometre is how many metres?
- Convert centimetres to metres, and vice versa; for example, 190 cm = 1.9 m.

Interactive whiteboard activity

Interactive whiteboard activity available to support this copymaster. See accompanying disk.

Main teaching activity

Equivalent lengths (page 43)

Additional activities suitable for developing the objectives

- Match abbreviations written onto cards (mm, cm, m, km, g, kg, mL, L) to words also written onto cards (millimetres, centimetres, metres, kilometres, grams, kilograms, millilitres, litres).
- Match equivalent measures written on cards; for example, 100 cm = 1 m. Play 'Snap' with these cards.
- Play 'Equivalent measures bingo'.
- Convert centimetres to metres, and vice versa; for example, 190 cm = 1.9 m.
- Measure the heights of five tall objects. Record their heights in cm and m. List the objects in order from shortest to tallest.

Answers

1. (a) mm (b) cm (c) m (d) km

2. (a) 10 (b) 100 (c) 1000

3. (a) millimetres, centimetres, metres, kilometres
   (b) millimetres, centimetres, metres, kilometres, miles

4. $^1/_{10}$ of 1 km = 100 m, $^1/_4$ of 1 km = 250 m, $^1/_2$ of 1 km = 500 m, $^3/_4$ of 1 km = 750 m, $^1/_{10}$ of 1 m = 10 cm, $^1/_4$ of 1 m = 25 cm, $^1/_2$ of 1 m = 50 cm, $^3/_4$ of 1 m = 75 cm

5. (a) 1.8 m (b) 2.37 m (c) 5.04 m
   (d) 9.2 m (e) 105 cm (f) 659 cm
   (g) 840 cm (h) 75 cm (i) 350 cm

Challenge: Teacher check

EQUIVALENT LENGTHS

1. Match the units of measure to the correct abbreviation.

   (a) millimetres •   • cm

   (b) centimetres •   • km

   (c) metres •   • mm

   (d) kilometres •   • m

2. Answer these statements.

   (a) There are _____ millimetres in 1 centimetre.

   (b) There are _____ centimetres in 1 metre.   (c) There are _____ metres in 1 kilometre.

3. (a) Write the four units of length in order of size, from smallest to largest.

metres	centimetres	kilometres	millimetres

   smallest ➞ _____ , _____ , _____ ,

   _____ ➞ largest.

   A mile is also a unit of length. It is more than 1 km but less than 2 km.

   (b) Write the five units of length in order of size, from smallest to largest.

metres	centimetres	miles	kilometres	millimetres

   smallest ➞ _____ , _____ , _____ ,

   _____ , _____ ➞ largest.

4. Match the equivalent lengths.

$\frac{1}{10}$ of 1 km	$\frac{1}{4}$ of 1 km	$\frac{1}{2}$ of 1 km	$\frac{3}{4}$ of 1 km	$\frac{1}{10}$ of 1 m	$\frac{1}{4}$ of 1 m	$\frac{1}{2}$ of 1 m	$\frac{3}{4}$ of 1 m

500 m	10 cm	750 m	75 cm	100 m	250 m	25 cm	50 cm

5. Convert the centimetres to metres, and vice versa.

   (a) 180 cm = _____ m   (b) 237 cm = _____ m   (c) 504 cm = _____ m

   (d) 920 cm = _____ m   (e) 1.05 m = _____ cm   (f) 6.59 m = _____ cm

   (g) 8.4 m = _____ cm   (h) 0.75 m = _____ cm   (i) 3.5 m = _____ cm

CHALLENGE On the back of the sheet, measure and record the height of five pupils. Write their heights in (a) metres (b) centimetres.

MEASURING

Objectives

- Choose and use standard metric units and their abbreviations when estimating, measuring and recording length.

- Use decimal notation to record measurements.

- Interpret intervals and divisions on partially numbered scales and record readings accurately, where appropriate to the nearest tenth of a unit.

Oral work and mental calculation

- Use the vocabulary: *millimetres, centimetres, metres, kilometres, ruler, metre stick, tape measure, trundle wheel, estimate, measure, length, width, height, distance, perimeter, longest, shortest, roughly, nearly, approximately, about.*

- Demonstrate how to measure using the scales on a ruler, metre stick, tape measure and trundle wheel.

- Ask pupils to estimate the length/width/height of an object and write their estimate on a piece of paper. Then measure the object to find the measurement. Which pupil made the closest estimate?

Interactive whiteboard activity

Interactive whiteboard activity available to support this copymaster. See accompanying disk.

Main teaching activity

Measuring in centimetres and metres (page 45)

Additional activities suitable for developing the objectives

- Use a ruler to draw lines to the nearest whole and half a centimetre. Extend to the nearest millimetre.

- Use a ruler to find and measure objects that are 5 cm, 10 cm and 20 cm in length. Record results in a simple table.

- Use a metre stick to find and measure objects that are 0.5 m, 1 m and 1.5 m in length. Record results in a simple table.

- Use a metre stick to measure the height of five classmates. Write the names and heights in order from shortest to tallest.

- Record lengths measured in metres and centimetres in decimal form; for example, 1.45 metres.

- Measure given items using a ruler, metre stick, tape measure or trundle wheel, as appropriate.

- Estimate measurements; for example, length of a reading book, and then measure, to check accuracy of estimate.

Answers

1. (a) 6.5 cm   (b) 3 cm   (c) 4.5 cm
   (d) 8.5 cm   (e) 1 cm

2. (a) 3.5 cm   (b) 4.5 cm
   (c) 2 cm   (d) 5.5 cm

3. Teacher check

Challenge: Teacher check

MEASURING IN CENTIMETRES AND METRES

1. Measure the lines below using your ruler.

   (a) ———————————————   = _____

   (b) ——————   = _____

   (c) ———————————   = _____

   (d) —————————————————————   = _____

   (e) ———   = _____

2. Measure the length of these leaves in centimetres.

   (a)  ☐ cm

   (b)  ☐ cm

   (c)   ☐ cm

   (d)  ☐ cm

3. Estimate then measure these objects in metres.

Object	Estimate		Measure
(a) Height of the classroom door.	Between ☐ m and	☐ m	m
(b) Length of the window.	Between ☐ m and	☐ m	m
(c) Width of the board.	Between ☐ m and	☐ m	m
(d) Width of your desk.	Between ☐ m and	☐ m	m
(e) Length of the corridor.	Between ☐ m and	☐ m	m

CHALLENGE Measure the height of five of your classmates in centimetres. On the back of this sheet, write their heights in order from the shortest to the tallest.

MEASURING

Objectives

*   Choose and use standard metric units and their abbreviations when estimating, measuring and recording length.
*   Know the meaning of kilo, centi and milli.

Oral work and mental calculation

*   Use the vocabulary: *millimetres, centimetres, metres, kilometres, ruler, metre stick, tape measure, trundle wheel, estimate, measure, length, width, height, distance, perimeter, longest, shortest, roughly, nearly, approximately, about.*

*   Give pupils a unit of length (mm, cm, m, km) and ask them to name something they could measure using that unit.

*   Give pupils an object; for example, length of a pencil sharpener, height of a lamp post, and ask them to say which unit they would use to measure it with; for example, mm, cm, m or km.

*   Give pupils a piece of measuring equipment (ruler, metre stick, tape measure, trundle wheel) and ask them to name something they could measure using that piece of equipment.

*   Give pupils an object; for example, length of a pencil sharpener, height of a window, and ask them to say which piece of equipment they would use to measure it with; for example, ruler, metre stick, tape measure, trundle wheel.

Interactive whiteboard activity

Interactive whiteboard activity available to support this copymaster. See accompanying disk.

Main teaching activity

Length – choosing formal units (page 47)

Additional activities suitable for developing the objectives

*   Draw and label items that you would measure using mm, cm, m and km.

*   Look through magazines and cut out pictures of items that you would measure using a ruler, metre stick, tape measure or trundle wheel. Make a poster showing what items you could measure using each piece of equipment.

Answers

1. (a) one thousand

    (b) one hundredth

    (c) one thousandth

2. (a) cm   (b) m   (c) m   (d) km
    (e) cm   (f) m   (g) m   (h) km

3. Teacher check

4. Ruler (red): length of a pencil, width of a maths book, length of a piece of lego™.

    Metre stick (blue): width of your classroom, height of a door.

    Tape measure (yellow): distance around a tree trunk, distance around your waist.

    Trundle wheel (green): length of the playground, perimeter of your school.

Challenge: h, d, g, f, b, c, a, e

1. Match each prefix to its meaning.

   (a) | kilo | •   • | one thousandth |

   (b) | centi | •   • | one thousand |

   (c) | milli | •   • | one hundredth |

2. Choose which formal unit of measurement you would use to measure these: cm, m or km.

   (a) The length of a pen _____

   (b) The height of the classroom _____

   (c) Your height _____

   (d) The distance between your home and school _____

   (e) The length of your scissors _____

   (f) The width of a tennis court _____

   (g) The height of a tall oak tree _____

   (h) The distance between Birmingham and Cardiff _____

3. Suggest two different items you would measure in ...

   (a) km _____ and _____

   (b) m _____ and _____

   (c) cm _____ and _____

   (d) mm _____ and _____

4. Colour each item according to the instrument you would use to measure it.

   Key

   ruler = red

   metre stick = blue

   tape measure = yellow

   trundle wheel = green

   | length of a pencil | length of the playground | distance around your waist |

   | distance around a tree trunk | width of your classroom | length of a piece of Lego™ |

   | width of a maths book | perimeter of your school | height of a door |

CHALLENGE On the back of this sheet, write the items in Question 2 in order from the longest to the shortest in length or distance.

MEASURING

Objectives

- Choose and use standard metric units and their abbreviations.

- Use decimal notation to record measurements.

Oral work and mental calculation

- Use the vocabulary: *gram, kilogram, millilitre, litre, pint.*

- Ask verbal equivalence questions; for example, 1000 millilitres is the same as how many litres? $^3/_4$ of 1 kilogram is how many grams?

- Convert grams to kilograms and millilitres to litres, and vice versa; for example, 5000 g = 5 kg.

Main teaching activity

Equivalent masses and capacities (page 49)

Additional activities suitable for developing the objectives

- Match abbreviations written onto cards (mm, cm, m, km, g, kg, mL, L) to words also written onto cards (millimetres, centimetres, metres, kilometres, grams, kilograms, millilitres, litres).

- Match equivalent measures written on cards; for example, 1000 g = 1 kg. Play 'Snap' with these cards.

- Play 'Equivalent measures bingo'.

- Convert grams to kilograms and millilitres to litres, and vice versa; for example, 5000 g = 5 kg.

- Measure the masses of five school bags. Record their masses in g and kg. List the school bags in order from lightest to heaviest.

- Measure the capacities of five containers. Record their capacities in mL and L. List the containers in order from smallest to largest capacity.

Answers

1. (a) g   (b) kg   (c) mL   (d) L

2. (a) 1000   (b) 1000

3. millilitre, pint, litre

4. $^1/_{10}$ of 1 kg = 100 g, $^1/_4$ of 1 kg = 250 g, $^1/_2$ of 1 kg = 500 g, $^3/_4$ of 1 kg = 750 g, $^1/_{10}$ of 1 L = 100 mL, $^1/_4$ of 1 L = 250 mL, $^1/_2$ of 1 L = 500 mL, $^3/_4$ of 1 L = 750 mL

5. (a) 4 kg   (b) 7.5 kg   (c) 8.75 kg   (d) 2500 g
   (e) 5800 g   (f) 6100 g   (g) 7400 g

6. (a) 3 L   (b) 4.25 L   (c) 9.5 L   (d) 6700 mL
   (e) 7500 mL   (f) 4200 mL   (g) 6600 mL

Challenge: Teacher check

EQUIVALENT MASSES AND CAPACITIES

1. Match the units of measure to the correct abbreviation.

   (a) grams   •   •   kg

   (b) kilograms   •   •   mL

   (c) millilitres   •   •   L

   (d) litres   •   •   g

2. Answer these statements.

   (a) There are _____ grams in 1 kilogram.   (b) There are _____ millilitres in 1 litre.

3.   **A pint is another measure of capacity. It is roughly equal to half a litre.**

   Write the three units of capacity in order of size, from smallest to largest.

pint   litre   millilitre

   smallest → _____ , _____ , _____ → largest.

4. Match the equivalent measurements.

$\frac{1}{10}$ of 1 kg	$\frac{1}{4}$ of 1 kg	$\frac{1}{2}$ of 1 kg	$\frac{3}{4}$ of 1 kg	$\frac{1}{10}$ of 1 L	$\frac{1}{4}$ of 1 L	$\frac{1}{2}$ of 1 L	$\frac{3}{4}$ of 1 L

500 g	250 mL	750 g	100 mL	100 g	750 mL	250 g	500 mL

5. Convert the grams to kilograms, and vice versa.

   (a) 4000 g = _____ kg

   (b) 7500 g = _____ kg

   (c) 8750 g = _____ kg

   (d) 2.5 kg = _____ g

   (e) 5.8 kg = _____ g

   (f) 6.1 kg = _____ g

   (g) 7.4 kg = _____ g

6. Convert the millilitres to litres, and vice versa.

   (a) 3000 mL = _____ L

   (b) 4250 mL = _____ L

   (c) 9500 mL = _____ L

   (d) 6.7 L = _____ mL

   (e) 7.5 L = _____ mL

   (f) 4.2 L = _____ mL

   (g) 6.6 L = _____ mL

CHALLENGE On the back of the sheet, weigh and record the mass of five books. Write the mass in (a) kilograms (b) grams.

MEASURING

Objectives

- Choose and use standard metric units and their abbreviations when estimating, measuring and recording weight.
- Use decimal notation to record measurements.
- Interpret intervals and divisions on partially numbered scales and record readings accurately.

Oral work and mental calculation

- Use the vocabulary: *grams, kilograms, balance scales, kitchen scales, bathroom scales, estimate, measure, mass, lightest, heaviest, roughly, nearly, approximately, about.*
- Give pupils a unit of mass (g/kg) and ask them to name something they could weigh using that unit. Give them a piece of measuring equipment; for example, balance scales, and ask them to name an object they could weigh using it.
- Give pupils an object; for example, pencil sharpener, sack of potatoes, and ask them to say which unit they would use to weigh it with; for example, g or kg. Then ask them to say which piece of equipment they would use to weigh it with; for example, kitchen scales, bathroom scales.
- Demonstrate how to measure mass using the scales on different weighing scales.
- Ask pupils to estimate the mass of an object and write their estimate on a piece of paper. Then weigh the object to find the mass. Which pupil made the closest estimate?

Interactive whiteboard activity

Interactive whiteboard activity available to support this copymaster. See accompanying disk.

Main teaching activity

Measuring in grams and kilograms (page 51)

Additional activities suitable for developing the objectives

- Draw and label items that you would weigh using g and kg.
- Look through magazines and cut out pictures of items that you would weigh using kitchen scales or bathroom scales. Make a poster showing what items you could weigh using each piece of equipment.
- Use weighing scales to find and weigh objects that are 500 g and 1 kg in mass. Record results in a simple table.
- Weigh five classmates. Write the names and masses in order from lightest to heaviest.
- Measure given items using kitchen or bathroom scales, as appropriate.
- Estimate weights and then measure, to check accuracy of estimate.

Answers

1. lollies = g, joint of meat = kg, pasta = g, nuts = g, cheese = g, tea = g, oranges = kg, jelly = g, rice = kg, potatoes = kg

2. Teacher check

3. Teacher check

Challenge: (a) kg (b) g (c) g (d) kg (e) g (f) kg (g) g

There are 1000 grams (g) in a kilogram (kg).

1. Label these items with g or kg.

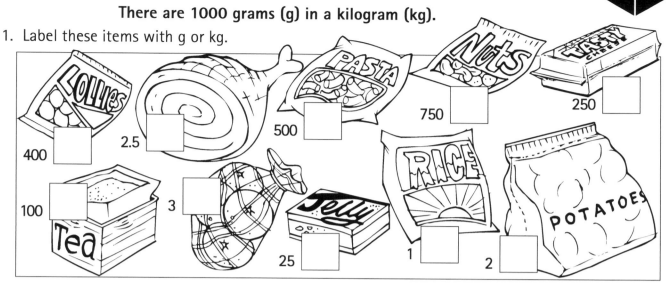

400   2.5   500   750   250

100   3   25   1   2

2. Estimate and weigh these objects using kitchen scales.

Object	Estimate				Measure
(a) scissors	Between		and		grams
					g
(b) banana	Between		and		grams
					g
(c) glue stick	Between		and		grams
					g
(d) orange	Between		and		grams
					g

3. Weigh yourself on bathroom scales and ask five other volunteer classmates to do the same. Record the weights in kilograms then order them from the lightest (a) to the heaviest (f).

Me (_____) = _____ kg

Person 1 (_____) = _____ kg

Person 2 (_____) = _____ kg

Person 3 (_____) = _____ kg

Person 4 (_____) = _____ kg

Person 5 (_____) = _____ kg

(a) _____ kg

(b) _____ kg

(c) _____ kg

(d) _____ kg

(e) _____ kg

(f) _____ kg

Write g or kg next to the objects to show the unit they would be measured in.

CHALLENGE

(a) a person _____   (b) loaf of bread _____   (c) a carrot _____   (d) a dog _____

(e) a packet of biscuits _____   (f) a bag of oranges _____   (g) a piece of cheese _____

MEASURING

Objectives

- Choose and use standard metric units and their abbreviations when estimating, measuring and recording capacity.

- Use decimal notation to record measurements.

- Interpret intervals and divisions on partially numbered scales and record readings accurately.

Oral work and mental calculation

- Use the vocabulary: *millilitres, litres, measuring jug, containers, estimate, measure, capacity, most, least, roughly, nearly, approximately, about.*

- Ask pupils to name items that need to be measured using capacity.

- Give pupils a container; for example, bucket, medicine bottle, and ask them to say which unit they would use to measure the capacity of it with; for example, mL or L. Then ask them to say which piece of equipment they would use to measure its capacity with; for example, a litre jug or 100 mL beaker.

- Demonstrate how to measure capacity using the scales on different measuring containers.

- Ask pupils to estimate the capacity of a container and write their estimate on a piece of paper. Then measure the container's capacity. Which pupil made the closest estimate?

Interactive whiteboard activity

Interactive whiteboard activity available to support this copymaster. See accompanying disk.

Main teaching activity

Measuring in millilitres and litres (page 53)

Additional activities suitable for developing the objectives

- Draw and label containers that you would measure the capacities of using mL and L.

- Find containers with capacities of 500 mL and 1 L. Record results in a simple table.

- Choose five containers. Order them from smallest to largest capacity.

- Estimate capacities and then measure, to check accuracy of estimate.

Answers

1. cream = mL
   ice-cream = L
   medicine = mL
   glue = mL
   dishwashing liquid = L
   chilli sauce = mL
   shampoo = mL
   petrol = L
   oil = mL

2. Teacher check

Challenge: Teacher check

MEASURING IN MILLILITRES AND LITRES

There are 1000 millilitres (mL) in 1 litre (L).

1. Write mL (millilitres) or L (litres) on these containers.

2. Estimate and then measure the capacities of these containers.

Container	Estimate					Measure
(a) yoghurt pot	Between		and		mL	mL
(b) cup	Between		and		mL	mL
(c) can of pop	Between		and		mL	mL
(d) storage box	Between		and		litres	litres
(e) bucket	Between		and		litres	litres
(f) rubbish bin	Between		and		litres	litres
(g) baby bath	Between		and		litres	litres

CHALLENGE Draw and label two items you would measure in millilitres and two items you would measure in litres.

millilitres	millilitres	litres	litres

Objectives • Identifies appropriate units of measurement.
• Estimates and measures capacities in mL and L. **Primary mathematics** Prim-Ed Publishing www.prim-ed.com **53**

MEASURING

Objective

• Interpret intervals and divisions on partially numbered scales and record readings accurately.

Oral work and mental calculation

• Demonstrate how to measure using the scales on different pieces of measuring equipment; for example, length (ruler/tape measure), mass (kitchen scales), capacity (litre jug) and temperature (thermometer).

• Show a metre stick with some numbers on the scale hidden. Pupils say what the hidden numbers are.

Interactive whiteboard activity

Interactive whiteboard activity available to support this copymaster. See accompanying disk.

Main teaching activity

Reading scales (page 55)

Additional activities suitable for developing the objective

• Practise measuring using a wide range of measuring equipment with a wide range of scales; for example, length (ruler/tape measure), mass (kitchen scales), capacity (litre jug) and temperature (thermometer).

• Estimate lengths, masses and capacities and then measure, to check accuracy of estimates.

• Write missing numbers onto drawings of scales with numbers missing.

Answers

1. (a) 35°C   (b) 55 cm
   (c) 125 mL   (d) 25 kg

2. 20, 30, 40, 60, 70, 80, 90

3. (a) 100 g   (b) 400 g
   (c) 900 g   (d) 600 g

4. (a) 150 mL   (b) 800 mL
   (c) 300 mL   (d) 1000 mL or 1 L

Challenge: Teacher check

READING SCALES

Not all numbers are included on scales and other measuring devices. A line in between two numbers represents the number halfway between the two.

1. What measurements are shown on these scales?

(a)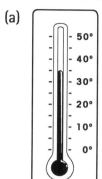

(b)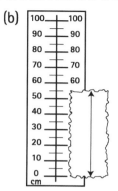

(c)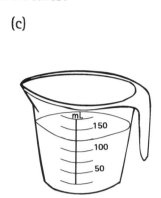

(d)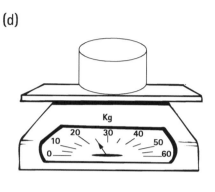

_____   _____   _____   _____

2. Fill in the missing numbers on this tape measure.

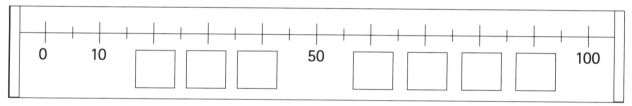

3. Write the weight shown on these kitchen scales.

(a)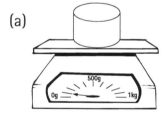

(b)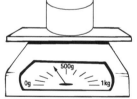

(c)

(d)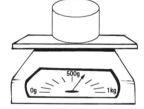

_____ g   _____ g   _____ g   _____ g

4. Write the amount shown on these jugs of water.

(a)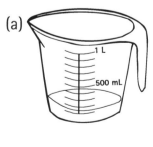

(b)

(c)

(d)

_____ mL   _____ mL   _____ mL   _____ mL

CHALLENGE Why do you think that not all numbers are included on measuring devices?

_____

MEASURING

Objective
- Measure and calculate the perimeter of rectangles.

Oral work and mental calculation
- Use the vocabulary: *perimeter, distance, edge, area, surface, covers, footsteps, hand spans, digits, strides, centimetres, square centimetres (cm²)*.

- Demonstrate how to measure the perimeter of a small object (e.g. book) using non-standard counting methods (e.g. paperclips, cubes).

- Demonstrate how to measure the perimeter of a larger object (e.g. table) using non-standard counting methods (e.g. hand spans).

- Give pupils a method of measuring using body parts; for example, digits, hand spans, strides. Ask pupils to say perimeters that could be measured using the body parts; for example, digits = pencil, strides = length of playground.

Main teaching activity
Perimeter – informal units (page 57)

Additional activities suitable for developing the objective
- Measure and record the perimeters of small objects using non-standard counting methods. Record results in a simple table.

- Measure and record the perimeters of larger objects using non-standard counting methods. Record results in a simple table.

- Order perimeters from smallest to largest, and vice versa.

- Draw around a square. Measure the perimeter in digits. Do the sides all have the same measurement?

- Draw around a rectangle. Measure the perimeter using paperclips. Do the two longer sides have the same measurement?

Answers
1. Teacher check
2. Teacher check
3. Teacher check
4. Teacher check

Challenge: Teacher check

PERIMETER – INFORMAL UNITS

Perimeter is the length or the distance around a shape or object.

1. Estimate and then measure the perimeter of these objects using cubes.

Object	Estimate			Measure
(a) calculator	Between		and	
(b) book	Between		and	
(c) envelope	Between		and	
(d) this worksheet	Between		and	

2. Estimate and then measure the perimeter of these objects using lolly sticks.

Object	Estimate			Measure
(a) your desk	Between		and	
(b) cloakroom	Between		and	
(c) classroom	Between		and	
(d) dining hall	Between		and	

3. Estimate and then measure the perimeter of the classroom using your feet.

Estimate: Between _____ and _____   Measure: _____ feet.

4. Estimate and then measure the perimeter of your desk top using your hand span.

Estimate: Between _____ and _____   Measure: _____ hand spans.

CHALLENGE Estimate and then measure the perimeter of a netball court using large steps/strides. Work with a partner.

Estimate: Between _____ and _____ steps   Measure: _____ steps

MEASURING

Objective
- Measure and calculate the perimeter of rectangles.

Oral work and mental calculation
- Use the vocabulary: *perimeter, distance, edge, area, surface, covers, footsteps, hand spans, digits, strides, centimetres, square centimetres (cm^2).*

- Demonstrate how to measure the perimeter of a rectangle drawn onto squared paper.

- Demonstrate how to measure the perimeter of a small object (e.g. book) using centimetres.

- Answer verbal questions involving perimeters; for example, The perimeter of a square is 24 cm. What length is each side of the square? How long is the perimeter of a 4 cm x 5 cm rectangle?

- Discuss and explain a short way to work out the perimeter of a rectangle.

Main teaching activity
Perimeter – formal units (page 59)

Additional activities suitable for developing the objective
- Estimate, measure and record the perimeters of small objects using centimetres. Record results in a simple table.

- Order perimeters from smallest to largest, and vice versa.

- Draw around a square. Measure the perimeter in centimetres. Do the sides all have the same measurement? Repeat for regular triangles and perimeters.

- Draw different rectangles onto squared paper. Measure the perimeters and write them into the middle of the shapes.

- Draw two shapes with a perimeter of 16 cm. Which has the largest area?

- Answer word problems involving perimeter; for example, A rectangular garden measures 15 m by 5 m. How many metres of fencing are needed to totally enclose the garden?

Answers
1. (a) 12 cm   (b) 9 cm
   (c) 17 cm   (d) 12 cm

2. Teacher check

Challenge: Teacher check

PERIMETER – FORMAL UNITS

1. Estimate and measure the perimeter of the shapes below in centimetres.

(a)

Estimate = _____ cm

Measure = _____ cm + _____ cm +

_____ cm + _____ cm

Perimeter = _____ cm

(b)
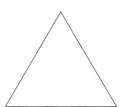

Estimate = _____ cm

Measure = _____ cm + _____ cm +

_____ cm

Perimeter = _____ cm

(c)

Estimate = _____ cm

Measure = _____ cm + _____ cm +

_____ cm + _____ cm

Perimeter = _____ cm

(d)

Estimate = _____ cm

Measure = _____ cm + _____ cm +

_____ cm + _____ cm

Perimeter = _____ cm

2. Working with a partner, use a trundle wheel to estimate and then measure the perimeter of these.

Object	Estimate		Measure
(a) netball court	Between [ ] m and	[ ] m	m
(b) football pitch	Between [ ] m and	[ ] m	m
(c) classroom building	Between [ ] m and	[ ] m	m

CHALLENGE

Working with a partner, estimate and then measure the perimeter of the school field or hall, using a trundle wheel.

Estimate: Between _____ and _____ m   Measure: _____ m

MEASURING

Objective
- Find the area of rectilinear shapes.

Oral work and mental calculation
- Use the vocabulary: *perimeter, distance, edge, area, surface, covers, footsteps, hand spans, digits, strides, centimetres, square centimetres (cm²).*
- Demonstrate how to measure the area of a small object (e.g. book) using non-standard counting methods (e.g. cubes).
- Demonstrate how to measure the area of a larger object (e.g. rug) using non-standard counting methods (e.g. sheets of newspaper).

Main teaching activity
Area – informal units (page 61)

Additional activities suitable for developing the objective
- Draw around a square. Measure the area using cubes. Repeat for a rectangle.
- Draw simple shapes on squared paper. Count the squares inside the shape to discover the area.
- Cover objects (e.g. greetings card) with a transparent squared grid and count the squares, to work out the area.
- Measure and record the areas of small objects using non-standard counting methods. Record results in a simple table.
- Measure and record the areas of larger objects using non-standard counting methods. Record results in a simple table.
- Order areas from smallest to largest, and vice versa.

Answers
1. Teacher check
2. Teacher check
3. Teacher check

Challenge: Teacher check

AREA – INFORMAL UNITS

Area is the space inside a shape or object.

1. Use cubes to estimate and measure the area of these objects.

Object	Estimate			Measure
(a) calculator	Between	and	cubes	cubes
(b) book	Between	and	cubes	cubes
(c) pencil case	Between	and	cubes	cubes
(d) dictionary	Between	and	cubes	cubes
(e) ruler	Between	and	cubes	cubes

2. Use large squares of paper to estimate and measure the area of these objects.

Object	Estimate			Measure
(a) desktop	Between	and	squares	squares
(b) window	Between	and	squares	squares
(c) half the board	Between	and	squares	squares
(d) chart (e.g. tables)	Between	and	squares	squares

3. Sketch a square about 2 cm by 2 cm.

CHALLENGE

Working with a partner, use large squares to estimate and then measure the area of the class pin-up/display board.

Estimate: Between _____ and _____ squares. Measure: _____ squares

MEASURING

Objective
- Find the area of rectilinear shapes drawn on a square grid by counting squares.

Oral work and mental calculation
- Use the vocabulary: *perimeter, distance, edge, area, surface, covers, footsteps, hand spans, digits, strides, centimetres, square centimetres (cm²).*

- Demonstrate how to measure the area of a small object (e.g. book) using squared centimetres.

- Demonstrate how to measure the area of a larger object (e.g. rug) using squared centimetres.

Main teaching activity
Measuring in square centimetres (page 63)

Additional activities suitable for developing the objective
- Draw simple shapes on squared paper. Count the squares inside the shape to discover the area.

- Cover objects (e.g. greetings card) with a transparent centimetre-squared grid and count the squares, to work out the area.

- Estimate, measure and record the areas of small objects using square centimetres. Record results in a simple table.

- Order areas from smallest to largest, and vice versa.

- Draw a range of different shapes, all with an area of 20 cm², onto squared paper. Measure the perimeter of each shape, and write it in the centre of the shape.

Answers
1. (a) 4 cm²   (b) 7 cm²   (c) 8 cm²   (d) 10 cm²
   (e) 9 cm²   (f) 6 cm²   (g) 5 cm²   (h) 12 cm²

2. a, g, f, b, c, e, d, h

3. Teacher check

Challenge: Teacher check

Area can be measured in square centimetres (cm²).

1. Find the area of the shapes below by counting the centimetre squares.

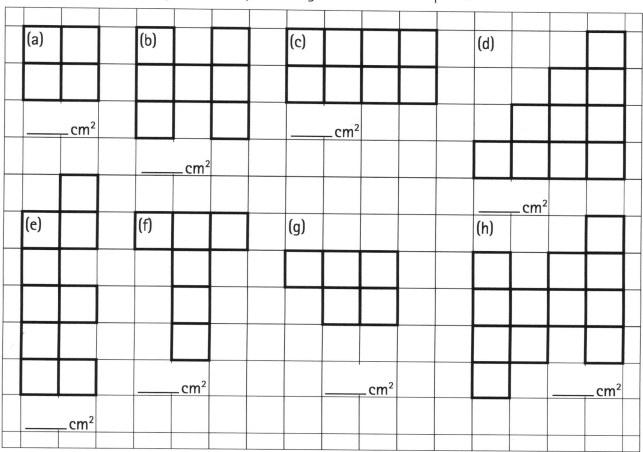

(a) _____ cm²

(b) _____ cm²

(c) _____ cm²

(d) _____ cm²

(e) _____ cm²

(f) _____ cm²

(g) _____ cm²

(h) _____ cm²

2. Order the shapes from the smallest to the largest.

_____ , _____ , _____ , _____ , _____ , _____ , _____ , _____ .

3. Trace an object of your choice below. Count the whole grid squares only to find its area.

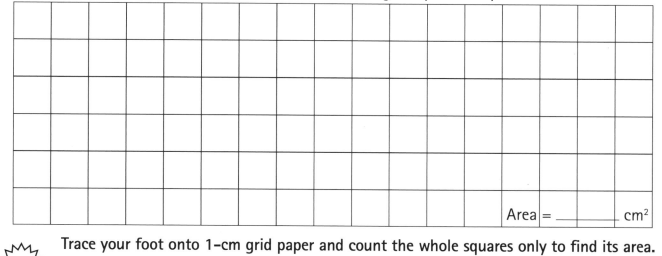

Area = _____ cm²

CHALLENGE Trace your foot onto 1–cm grid paper and count the whole squares only to find its area.

Area = _____ cm²

MEASURING

Objectives

- Measure and calculate the perimeter of rectangles.

- Find the area of rectilinear shapes drawn on a square grid by counting squares.

Oral work and mental calculation

- Use the vocabulary: *perimeter, distance, edge, area, surface, covers, footsteps, hand spans, digits, strides, centimetres, square centimetres (cm²).*

- Demonstrate how to measure the perimeter and area of a small object (e.g. book) using centimetres and squared centimetres.

- Demonstrate how to measure the perimeter and area of a larger object (e.g. rug) using centimetres and squared centimetres.

Interactive whiteboard activity

Interactive whiteboard activity available to support this copymaster. See accompanying disk.

Main teaching activity

Area and perimeter (page 65)

Additional activities suitable for developing the objectives

- Draw simple shapes on squared paper. Count the squares inside the shape to discover the area and count the squares around the outside of the shape to discover the perimeter.

- Estimate, measure and record the areas and perimeters of small objects using square centimetres and centimetres. Record results in a simple table.

- Order perimeters and areas from smallest to largest, and vice versa.

- Draw a range of different shapes, all with a given area, onto squared paper. Measure the perimeter of each shape, and write it in the centre of the shape.

- Draw a range of different shapes, all with a given perimeter, onto squared paper. Measure the area of each shape, and write it in the centre of the shape.

Answers

1. (a) A = 8 cm², P = 12 cm
   (b) A = 9 cm², P = 12 cm
   (c) A = 12 cm², P = 16 cm
   (d) A = 12 cm², P = 16 cm

2. Teacher check

Challenge: Teacher check

1. Find the area and perimeter of these shapes. Count the inside squares to find the area and the squares around the edge of the shape to find the perimeter.

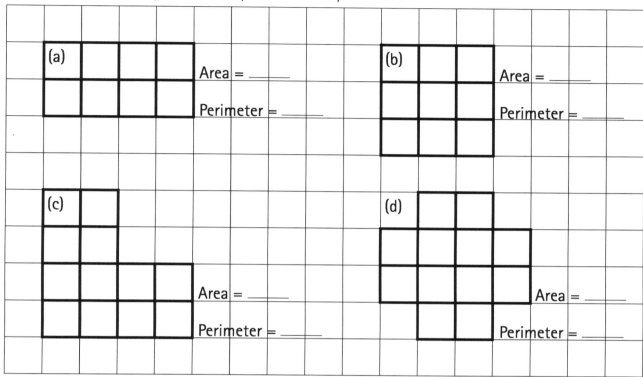

(a) Area = _____ Perimeter = _____

(b) Area = _____ Perimeter = _____

(c) Area = _____ Perimeter = _____

(d) Area = _____ Perimeter = _____

2. Trace one hand below (fingers together). Then count the whole inside squares to find its area and the outside squares to find its perimeter.

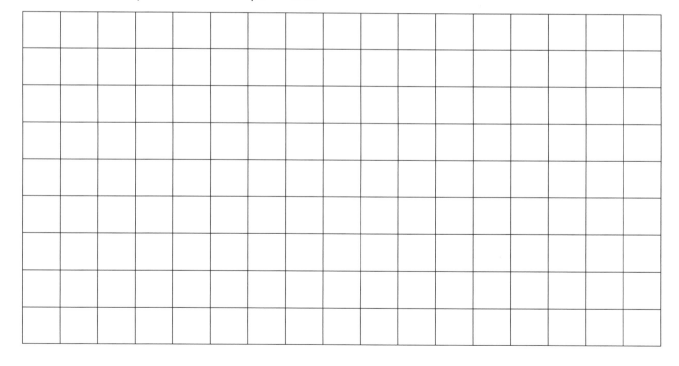

CHALLENGE Use cubes to find the area and perimeter of a dictionary.

Area = _____ cubes. Perimeter = _____ cubes.

MEASURING

Objective
- Choose units of time to measure time intervals.

Oral work and mental calculation
- Use the vocabulary: *days of the week, months of the year, seasons, day, week, fortnight, month, year, leap year, century, millennium, morning, a.m., afternoon, evening, night, p.m., midnight, noon, second, minute, hour, today, tomorrow, yesterday, weekday, weekend, faster, slower, earliest, latest.*

- Answer questions; for example, How many seasons in one year? How many seconds in one minute? How many years in one century?

- Suggest things that they do that can be measured in seconds, minutes or hours.

- Discuss suitable units of time to measure: How long it takes to drink a glass of water, How long it takes to fly from England to Australia.

- Pupils vote for the most sensible suggestion in multiple choice activities; for example, Does a full kettle boil in about 3 seconds, 3 minutes or 30 minutes?

Main teaching activity
Periods of time (page 67)

Additional activities suitable for developing the objective
- Write a list of things that could be measured in seconds, minutes, hours, days, weeks, months and years.

- Use a stopwatch. Estimate and then time how many times tasks can be completed in one minute; for example, How many times can they write their name? How many star jumps can they do? How many times can they say 'I love you!' to their teacher?

- Use a stopwatch to time running races in PE lessons.

- Investigate how long they have lived. How many years? How many months? How many weeks?

Answers
1. Answers may vary:
   - (a) a few minutes
   - (b) about an hour
   - (c) a few minutes
   - (d) about an hour
   - (e) about half an hour
   - (f) several hours

2. d, b, f, c, a, e

Challenge: Teacher check

PERIODS OF TIME

1. Estimate the time it takes to complete the tasks below. Use phrases such as 'a few minutes', 'half an hour', 'less than an hour', 'about an hour', 'more than an hour' or 'several hours'.

2. Order these activities from taking the shortest time (1) to the longest time (6).

(a) school lunchtime ☐   (b) brushing your hair ☐   (c) eating dinner ☐

(d) flushing the toilet ☐   (e) sleeping at night ☐   (f) running a lap of the field ☐

 CHALLENGE On the back of this sheet, write three things that take you less than one hour to do and three things that take you longer than one hour to do.

MEASURING

Objective

- Choose units of time to measure time intervals.

Oral work and mental calculation

- Use the vocabulary: *days of the week, months of the year, seasons, day, week, fortnight, month, year, leap year, century, millennium, morning, a.m., afternoon, evening, night, p.m., midnight, noon, second, minute, hour, today, tomorrow, yesterday, weekday, weekend, faster, slower, earliest, latest.*

- Answer questions; for example, How many seasons in one year? How many seconds in one minute? How many years in one century?

- Suggest things that they do that can be measured in seconds, minutes or hours.

- Discuss suitable units of time to measure: How long it takes to drink a glass of water, How long it takes to fly from England to Australia.

- Pupils vote for the most sensible suggestion in multiple choice activities; for example, Does a full kettle boil in about 3 seconds, 3 minutes or 30 minutes?

Main teaching activity

Estimating and classifying time (page 69)

Additional activities suitable for developing the objective

- Write a list of things that could be measured in seconds, minutes, hours, days, weeks, months and years.

- Use a stopwatch. Estimate and then time how many times tasks can be completed in one minute; for example, How many times can they write their name? How many star jumps can they do? How many times can they say 'I love you!' to their teacher?

- Use a stopwatch to time running races in PE lessons.

- Investigate how long they have lived. How many years? How many months? How many weeks?

Answers

1. Teacher check
2. Teacher check

Challenge: Teacher check

1. Think about how long it takes you to do things, then write five different activities under each heading.

(a) about 10 seconds	(b) about 10 minutes	(c) about half an hour	(d) about 1 hour

2. Illustrate and describe something that takes you the following lengths of time to do.

(a) a few minutes

_____

_____

_____

(b) about an hour

_____

_____

_____

(c) a few hours

_____

_____

_____

 CHALLENGE Use an egg timer or the second hand on a clock to time how long it takes you to (a) jump 20 times, (b) write the 9 times table, (c) build a tower 10 blocks high.

MEASURING

Objectives
- Read time to the nearest minute.
- Use 12-hour clock notation.

Oral work and mental calculation
- Use the vocabulary: *morning, a.m., afternoon, evening, night, p.m., midnight, noon, second, minute, hour, o'clock, quarter past, half past, quarter to, analogue, digital.*
- Answer questions; for example, How many seconds in one minute? How many minutes in quarter of an hour?
- Practise reading time to the nearest minute on large analogue and digital clocks.
- Look at the classroom clock at given times of the school day and read the time.

Interactive whiteboard activity
Interactive whiteboard activity available to support this copymaster. See accompanying disk.

Main teaching activity
Analogue time (page 71)

Additional activities suitable for developing the objectives
- Write the time to the nearest minute on drawings of analogue and digital clocks.
- Match cards showing analogue times with cards showing equivalent digital times. Sort the cards according to whether they show a 'past' or 'to' time. Play 'Snap' to match each analogue time to its corresponding digital time.
- Write/Say times in different formats; for example, 8:44 = 44 minutes past 8 = 16 minutes to 9.

Answers
1. (a) 5:00   (b) 11:15   (c) 9:30   (d) 3:45
    (e) 2:35   (f) 11:55   (g) 9:18   (h) 7:26
    (i) 9:39   (j) 8:33

2. Teacher check

Challenge: Teacher check

1. Write the time shown on these clocks.

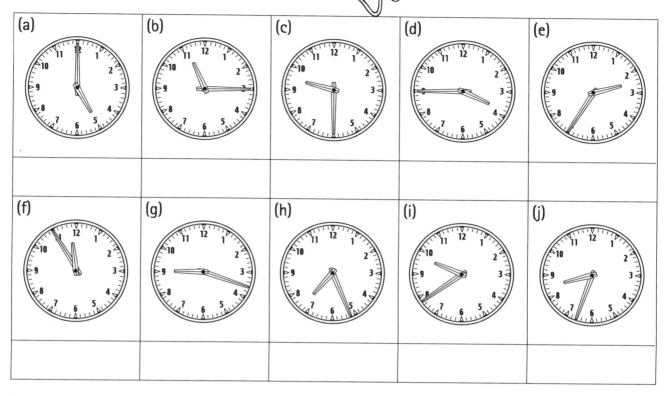

(a)	(b)	(c)	(d)	(e)
(f)	(g)	(h)	(i)	(j)

2. Draw the time on these clocks.

(a)	(b)	(c)	(d)	(e)
4 o'clock	quarter to 2	half past 7	10 past 4	5 to 7
(f)	(g)	(h)	(i)	(j)
3:34	7:52	1:27	10:18	5:08

CHALLENGE On a school day, at approximately what time do you have ...

breakfast? _____ break? _____ lunch? _____ dinner? _____

MEASURING

Objectives
- Read time to the nearest minute.
- Use 12-hour clock notation.

Oral work and mental calculation
- Use the vocabulary: *morning, a.m., afternoon, evening, night, p.m., midnight, noon, second, minute, hour, o'clock, quarter past, half past, quarter to, analogue, digital.*
- Answer questions; for example, How many seconds in one minute? How many minutes in quarter of an hour?
- Practise reading time to the nearest minute on large analogue and digital clocks.
- Look at a digital clock at given times of the school day and read the time.

Interactive whiteboard activity
Interactive whiteboard activity available to support this copymaster. See accompanying disk.

Main teaching activity
Digital time (page 73)

Additional activities suitable for developing the objectives
- Write the time to the nearest minute on drawings of analogue and digital clocks.
- Match cards showing analogue times with cards showing equivalent digital times. Sort the cards according to whether they show a 'past' or 'to' time. Play 'Snap' to match each analogue time to its corresponding digital time.
- Write/Say times in different formats; for example, 8:44 = 44 minutes past 8 = 16 minutes to 9.

Answers
1. (a) 9 o'clock   (b) 25 past 2
   (c) 5 past 10   (d) 22 minutes past 7
   (e) 23 minutes to 12   (f) 18 minutes to 7
   (g) 12 minutes past 1   (h) 2 minutes to 3

2. (a) 7:23   (b) 4:18   (c) 10:45   (d) 9:37
   (e) 12:09   (f) 1:25   (g) 3:52   (h) 6:40

Challenge: (a) 5:43 (b) 10:31 (c) 1:22

1. Write the time shown on these digital clocks using words.

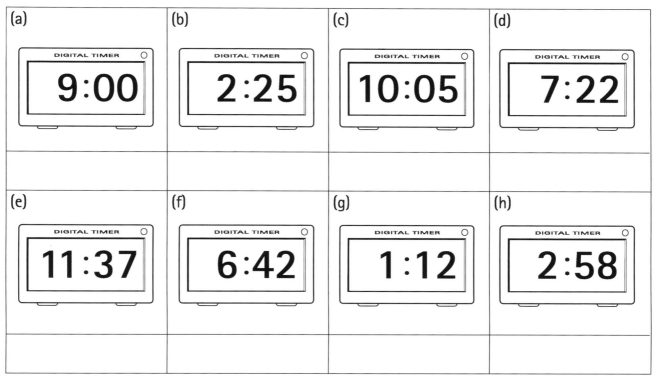

2. Write the digital time on the clock faces.

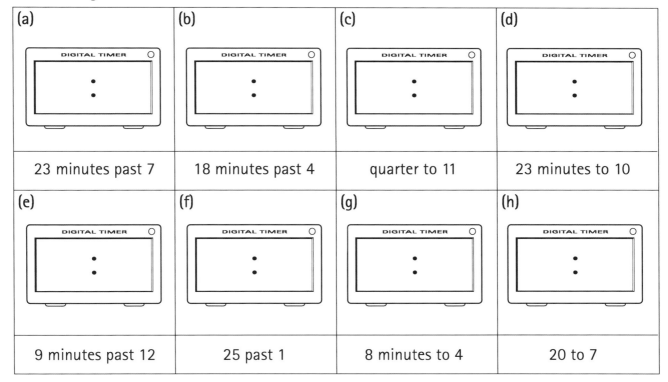

Write the digital times for each of these.

(a) five forty-three _____ (b) ten thirty-one _____ (c) one twenty-two _____

TEACHER INFORMATION

MEASURING

Objective
- Use a.m., p.m. and 12-hour clock notation.

Oral work and mental calculation
- Use the vocabulary: *morning, a.m., afternoon, evening, night, p.m., midnight, noon, second, minute, hour, o'clock, quarter past, half past, quarter to, analogue, digital.*
- Answer questions; for example, How many seconds in one minute? How many minutes in quarter of an hour?
- Practise reading time to the nearest minute on large analogue and digital clocks.
- Look at the classroom clock at given times of the school day and read the time.
- List things that pupils do in the morning (a.m.), afternoon (p.m.) and evening (p.m.).

Main teaching activity
Describing time (page 75)

Additional activities suitable for developing the objective
- Write the time to the nearest minute on drawings of analogue and digital clocks.
- Match cards showing analogue times with cards showing equivalent digital times. Sort the cards according to whether they show a 'past' or 'to' time. Play 'Snap' to match each analogue time to its corresponding digital time.
- Write/Say times in different formats; for example, 8:44 = 44 minutes past 8 = 16 minutes to 9.
- Draw and label things that they do in the morning (a.m.), afternoon (p.m.) and evening (p.m.).

Answers
1. (a) p.m.   (b) a.m.   (c) p.m.   (d) a.m.
   (e) a.m./p.m. (f) p.m.   (g) a.m.   (h) p.m.

2. (a) a.m./p.m. (b) p.m.
   (c) a.m./p.m. (d) a.m./p.m.
   (e) a.m./p.m. (f) p.m.

Challenge: Teacher check

DESCRIBING TIME

Time can be described as a.m. (from 12 midnight to 12 midday) or p.m. (from 12 midday to 12 midnight).

1. Write a.m. or p.m. beside these events.

    (a)   playing after school   _____

    (b)   getting ready for school   _____

    (c)   eating dinner   _____

    (d)   morning break   _____

    (e)   having a shower/bath   _____

    (f)   going to bed   _____

    (g)   waking up   _____

    (h)   leaving school   _____

2. Write a.m. or p.m. below these pictures. (Some could have more than one answer.)

⭐ CHALLENGE On the back of this sheet, write something you do on a weekend in the a.m. or p.m.

| Objective | *Identifies times of events according to a.m. or p.m.* | **Primary mathematics** | Prim-Ed Publishing www.prim-ed.com | 75 |

MEASURING

Objectives

- Read time to the nearest minute.

- Use a.m., p.m. and 12-hour clock notation.

- Calculate time intervals.

Oral work and mental calculation

- Use the vocabulary: *morning, a.m., afternoon, evening, night, p.m., midnight, noon, second, minute, hour, o'clock, quarter past, half past, quarter to, analogue, digital.*

- Answer questions; for example, How many seconds in one minute? How many minutes in quarter of an hour?

- Practise reading time to the nearest minute on large analogue and digital clocks.

- Look at the classroom clock at given times of the school day and read the time.

- List things that pupils do in the morning (a.m.), afternoon (p.m.) and evening (p.m.).

Main teaching activity

Analogue and digital time (page 77)

Additional activities suitable for developing the objectives

- Write the time to the nearest minute on drawings of analogue and digital clocks.

- Match cards showing analogue times with cards showing equivalent digital times. Sort the cards according to whether they show a 'past' or 'to' time. Play 'Snap' to match each analogue time to its corresponding digital time.

- Write/Say times in different formats; for example, 8:44 = 44 minutes past 8 = 16 minutes to 9.

- Draw and label things that they do in the morning (a.m.), afternoon (p.m.) and evening (p.m.).

Answers

1. (a) 7 minutes past 8, 8:07
   (b) 23 minutes past 2, 2:23
   (c) 22 minutes to 11, 10:38
   (d) 6 minutes to 1, 12:54

2. (a) Teacher check, 3:30
   (b) Teacher check, 11:25
   (c) Teacher check, 12:53
   (d) Teacher check, 6:18

3. (a) 8.55 a.m.   (b) 4.07 p.m.
   (c) 10.24 a.m.   (d) 3.37 p.m.
   (e) 5.35 p.m.

4. Teacher check

Challenge: (a) 6.27 p.m. (b) 10.51 a.m. (c) 4.05 p.m.
(d) 5.19 a.m. (e) 2.20 a.m.

ANALOGUE AND DIGITAL TIME

1. Write the analogue time and digital time shown on these clocks.

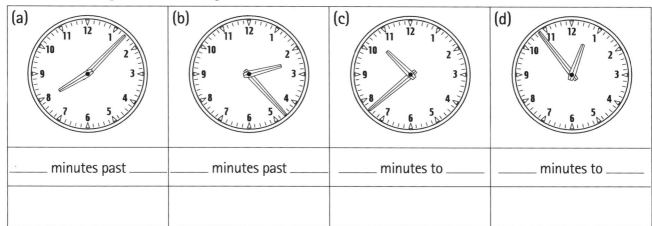

(a)	(b)	(c)	(d)
_____ minutes past _____	_____ minutes past _____	_____ minutes to _____	_____ minutes to _____

2. Draw the times on these clock faces and fill in the digital times.

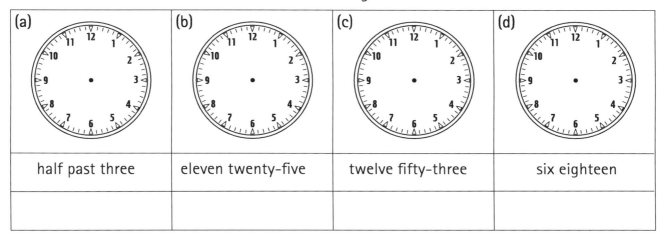

(a)	(b)	(c)	(d)
half past three	eleven twenty-five	twelve fifty-three	six eighteen

3. Match the times to the 'What am I?' clues.

(a) I am five minutes before 9.00 a.m.   •   •   3.37 p.m.

(b) I am seven minutes past 4.00 p.m.   •   •   5.35 p.m.

(c) I am two hours after 8.24 a.m.   •   •   8.55 a.m.

(d) I am three hours after 12.37 p.m.   •   •   4.07 p.m.

(e) I am twenty-five minutes before 6.00 p.m.   •   •   10.24 a.m.

4. Write a digital time to show when you usually:

(a) wake up on Sunday _____   (b) go to bed on Tuesday _____

(c) eat lunch on Saturday _____   (d) watch TV on Friday _____

What time will it be 4 hours after these times? (a) 2.27 p.m. _____

CHALLENGE

(b) 6.51 a.m. _____   (c) 12.05 p.m. _____   (d) 1.19 a.m. _____   (e) 10.20 p.m. _____

MEASURING

Objectives

- Use a.m., p.m. and 12-hour clock notation.
- Calculate time intervals from timetables.

Oral work and mental calculation

- Use the vocabulary: *morning, a.m., afternoon, evening, night, p.m., midnight, noon, second, minute, hour, o'clock, quarter past, half past, quarter to, analogue, digital.*

- Look at and discuss a large-format class timetable. Discuss how long you spend on different subjects in one week, which days different lessons are on, what lessons are in mornings or afternoons and how long breaks are for.

- Look at and discuss a simple large-format bus timetable. Discuss how many buses run, what time they leave and arrive, how long they take and how many stops they make. Answer verbal questions about the timetable; for example, I need to get to X by 10 a.m. What bus do I need to take? How long does the bus take to get from X to Y?

Interactive whiteboard activity

Interactive whiteboard activity available to support this copymaster. See accompanying disk.

Main teaching activity

Reading timetables (page 79)

Additional activities suitable for developing the objectives

- Use a TV guide to answer given questions; for example, What is your favourite TV programme? What days is it on? How long is it on for?

- Write a 'dream' TV guide for one day, which only shows pupil's favourite TV programmes.

- Look at simple bus or train timetables and answer given questions about them in writing.

Answers

1. (a) 5.30 a.m.   (b) 5.50 a.m.
    (c) 6.10 a.m.   (d) 6.45 a.m.
    (e) 6.30 a.m.   (f) 6.35 a.m.
    (g) 30 minutes   (h) 20 minutes
    (i) 10 minutes   (j) 30 minutes
    (k) 30 minutes   (l) second train

Challenge: 7.00 a.m., 7.30 a.m.

1. Look at the train timetable and answer the questions below.

Station	Departure times		
	first train	second train	third train
Eltham	5.30 a.m.	6.00 a.m.	6.30 a.m.
Montmorency	5.35 a.m.	6.05 a.m.	6.35 a.m.
Greensborough	5.40 a.m.	6.10 a.m.	6.40 a.m.
Watsonia	5.45 a.m.	6.15 a.m.	6.45 a.m.
Macleod	5.50 a.m.	6.20 a.m.	6.50 a.m.
Rosanna	5.55 a.m.	6.25 a.m.	6.55 a.m.
Heidelberg	6.00 a.m.	6.30 a.m.	7.00 a.m.

(a) What time does the first train depart Eltham? _____

(b) What time does the first train depart Macleod? _____

(c) What time does the second train depart Greensborough? _____

(d) What time does the third train depart Watsonia? _____

(e) What time does the second train depart Heidelberg? _____

(f) What time does the third train depart Montmorency? _____

(g) How long does it take the train to travel from Eltham to Heidelberg? _____

(h) How long does it take the train to travel between Montmorency and Rosanna? _____

(i) How long does it take the train to travel between Macleod and Heidelberg? _____

(j) How long between the first train departing Eltham and the second train? _____

(k) How long between the second train departing Watsonia and the third train? _____

(l) Which train would you catch if you had to leave Greensborough at 6.10 a.m.? _____

If a fourth train was running, what time would it depart Eltham? _____

What time would it arrive in Heidelberg? _____